pray
all
ways

May
My
prayer
Rise
like
Incense
before
You

PRAY ALL WAYS

WRITTEN AND ILLUSTRATED
BY
EDWARD HAYS

Forest of Peace
P u b l i s h i n g

Suppliers for the Spiritual Pilgrim

Other Books by the Author:
(available from the publisher)

Prayers and Rituals
Prayers for a Planetary Pilgrim
Prayers for the Domestic Church
Prayers for the Servants of God

Contemporary Spirituality
Holy Fools & Mad Hatters
A Pilgrim's Almanac
In Pursuit of the Great White Rabbit
The Lenten Labyrinth
Secular Sanctity

Parables and Stories
St. George and the Dragon
The Magic Lantern
The Ethiopian Tattoo Shop
Twelve and One-Half Keys
Sundancer
The Christmas Eve Storyteller

PRAY ALL WAYS

copyright © 1981, by Edward M. Hays

Library of Congress Catalog Card Number: 81-69329
ISBN: 0-939516-01-2

published by
Forest of Peace Publishing, Inc.
PO Box 269
Leavenworth, KS 66048-0269 USA

printed by
Hall Directory, Inc.
Topeka, KS 66608

1st Printing: October 1981
2nd Printing: June 1984
3rd Printing: May 1986
4th Printing: July 1988
5th Printing: September 1989
6th Printing: January 1991
7th Printing: January 1992
8th Printing: December 1993

cover designs by
Edward Hays

Dedicated

to the Shantivanam Community —

Jennifer Sullivan

Thomas Skorupa

Joanne Meyer

Thomas Turkle

Sr. Helen Miljour

David DeRusseau

and all former members

— who helped to live this book

before it was ever written.

October 17, 1981

contents

A Letter to the Reader

Like a Conversation

Dear Reader,

The reading of any book should be a dialogue between the reader and the author. If it is to be a real conversation, you, the reader, must not take a purely passive position, but should in some way respond to the ideas that are being shared. You can do this by saying to yourself: "Hmm, that's interesting! I never thought about that before." Another way is to have a pencil nearby and write your thoughts, ideas or objections along the margins. You may also wish to underscore those passages you want to return to or remember. To assist you in making the reading of this book a conversation between the two of us, generous margins have been allowed in the printing of the text. May this extra white space encourage you to respond by voice or by writing.

On how to live what you read

In the publishing of this book, it was also my intention that it be more than a book about prayer, but that it might also be a *prayer book*. The prayers found at the end of each chapter were written to encourage you to spend some time in reflective thought or prayer about the ideas presented in that chapter. These formal prayers are intended to be doorways to a daily living of prayer, rather than rote exercises of prayer.

The work of publishing this book was made easier by the kind assistance of good friends. I wish to express my personal gratitude to Betsy Evans who typed this and other manuscripts. She and Duane Evans have, by their friendship and support over the years, encouraged such ventures as this book.

My deep appreciation also goes to Steve and Cliff Hall of Hall Directory, Inc., the printers of this book, for their creative suggestions and craftsmanship.

And may I thank you, the reader, for joining me as, through the marvel of the printed word, we together explore the Invisible, the Divine Mystery.

PEACE

Edward Hays

October 17, 1981

introduction

To pray all ways is the unspoken admonition that is cleverly hidden in the spoken request of Jesus, "Pray always." To learn how to "pray always" is to master the art of learning how to pray in all ways and at all times. This does not mean that we must enter some remote and secluded monastery but rather that we must find a new definition of prayer. To pray has, over the centuries, meant to engage in vocal or in silent prayers. Praying has meant being faithful to special times of prayer that are set aside from the daily routines of life. But surely Jesus has not called all His followers to abandon all other activities of family, life and work to continually and solely engage in such times of prayer. What He does call us to is a life lived in communion with Him and with His Father. That living-communion is itself prayer, prayer which permeates all we engage in. It is the highest form of prayer to which we give the name of contemplation. Are we not all called to live out such a prayer, the prayer of contemplation?

This book is an attempt to speak about ways in which we can pray all ways. We will consider in the following pages how we can pray with our eyes, with our nose, our feet — and at those times we might not think were prayerful. To pray all ways is to find oneself involved in prayerful communion with God while feasting and fasting, while having fun and at play, while playing the fool and even while crying. The different activities of our daily lives are not distractions from prayer but rather the rich soil for prayer.

Such environmental and around-the-clock praise and prayer requires various virtues. It requires that we learn how to transform the mysteries of pain and suffering into worship. To pray all ways will call for a renewed sense of patience — the test of inner, or spiritual, balance for those who wish to become artists of prayer. Simplicity is also a necessary ingredient in both our lifestyles and in our prayer expressions, since it allows us the freedom necessary to be in touch with our inner selves and with the Spirit of the God of Love as well. Since prayer is the experience of, as well as the preparation for, the coming of the Kingdom, it is also a form of compassionate service. All communion with God leads us to behave like gods, to be compassionate. Our work becomes apostolic not simply because we place a name tag on our activities that says "this is apostolic," but because it is in the living tradition of the apostles. They were men of prayer who lived out the admonition of their Spiritual Master and Lord to "pray always" — and all ways. When prayer becomes the pattern for all that we do, then we will find that compassionate service will be natural to us. Until we have learned how to pray all ways the danger is that we will replace prayer with work and some acts of kindness. But if these activities, regardless of how much good seems to be happening, are separated from a heart that is praying, they cease to be apostolic, fruitful and redemptive. They become simply good deeds.

May this book awaken your heart to all the different ways in which you can pray as you care for your home, go about your daily work and live out your unique vocation. It is only a beginning; may it be a pattern for prayer that knows no hour or day but is alive always.

A Natural Spirituality

If prayer is considered only an indoor activity we shall miss out on the opportunity to worship in the most beautiful temple ever created: the cosmos. To pray all ways with nature will require that we are able to enter into creation, the earth and all its mysteries. But prayer and worship are also activities that cause us to look skyward, heavenward. We are, as a result, fond of ascensions.

In the world's religions we find a variety of holy ascensions. Christianity has the Ascension of Jesus and also the Assumption of the Blessed Mother Mary. In Judaism we find the Ascension of the prophet Elijah in his fiery chariot. Isalm celebrates the Ascension of Mohammed from the rock of Abraham in Jerusalem. That same upward movement appears in the stories of ancient Greece. Here, a young man named Icarus and his father, Daedalus, wanted to escape from the island of Crete. Daedalus fashioned for him wings from wax and feathers. He cautioned his son not to fly too high, but Icarus failed to heed the warning. The sun melted the wax and poor Icarus fell to his death. Perhaps we earthen folk long to imitate these upward departures from our earth, and this may explain the global fascination with ascending.

This same vertical ascendent fascination is found in a modern myth, the TV program *Star Trek*. Here, as in numerous other science fiction stories, humans escape from the earth with rockets to seek a more perfect Earth in space. We all long to rise above our nature and to be free of its laws and limitations. We experience anguish because we are mere earthlings. We also feel the pain of our human nature.

The source of that pain is complex. With our minds we are able to create beauty, to soar to the most distant star or even explore the hearts of atoms. With our imaginations we are able to create entire worlds and travel to them. Yet this marvelous mind is part of a body that will one day become the food of worms! The mind and the spirit are almost unlimited while the body is cramped with limitations. Our minds play in the stars while our bodies age, wrinkle and are dying. To reflect at all upon this paradox is to experience anguish and pain. As a result, we usually do not think about it! Instead we dream of finding power or magic with which to manipulate nature or control it for our own egotistical needs. Today, we attempt to escape from nature and its laws not with some wax and feathers but through science and technology.

We seem to constantly reject our earthen beginnings as we continuously attempt to "improve" on nature. We reject the ancient story of how Adam was made from clay, that he arose from the rich fabric of nature. Our pride or shame causes us to turn away from such a dirty story. Daily we seek to rise above our dusty beginnings and our earthen limitations. Each day, however, some government agency reports that this or that "improvement" on nature is harmful, if not lethal, to our health. This dream of escaping "up, up and away" from the earth is at the heart of numerous modern problems that arise from our divorce. What divorce? The separation between ourselves and nature. Pollution and various other environmental evils are not the only results of this divorce; our spiritual lives also bear numerous deep scars. These conditions are the result of a desire to live "above" nature instead of "in harmony" with it. But how can we find true holiness if we are rejecting our human nature? How can we, as citizens of a modern world, find a way to return to a life of harmony with all creation?

One way might be to create a new holy day! We could call this new religious holiday "The Feast of the Descension." Such a feast would not be the celebration of the Holy Ones, but rather a celebration of a necessary attitude within our own lives.

The Descent into Nature would be a festival to celebrate our "return" to the earth and its ancient "wholiness." Such a holy day could be an outdoor liturgy to mark the necessity of a return to a life lived in harmony with all creation; human nature and Nature living together in communion — not competition. Our imaginations could really play with numerous possibilities of such a feast. Song writers could compose special music for the day, with such lyrics as "O Come All Ye Faithful. Park your rocket ships, take off your shoes and socks. Wiggle your toes in the mud and remember, Children of God, from where you have come." The possibilities for such a celebration of "Our Descension into the Earth" are, indeed, unlimited.

The idea of such a festival as the "Descension" is only one way of awakening our hearts to the necessity of a relationship with nature as part of a healthy and holy pathway to God. Such a spirituality

15

would always be a home-coming. A *natural* spirituality seeks a return to that ageless friendship with creation that shows itself in a reverence for all nature.

Such a natural spirituality embraces the natural part of human nature instead of attempting to escape or suppress it. Whenever we reject our human nature (our bodies, sexuality, emotions), we also reject the God who created us as cosmic amphibians, as people intended to live in two worlds as one. Balance and harmony are holiness; they invite an awareness that all creation is good and therefore holy. The final word was the last sentence spoken by God at the end of each day of creation, "That's good!" True goodness, holiness, is the result of a balance between the inner and the outer person, between Nature and human nature, and between the Divine and the human, which exists within each of us.

The life of Jesus, His words, all reflect that He was living such a harmony with nature, self and God, His Father. As the new Adam, part of His work was to balance earth and heaven in a single existence. He was to live in the middle of a new garden, which was the earth, and to live there in peace and communion.

The yoga, or union, of His path was a union of earth and heaven, wine and bread, salt and oil, fire and water, sexuality and sanctity, death and life . . . and God and ourselves. Such a natural spirituality will not be easy for us electric, air-conditioned, plastic-loving, comfort-seeking people. To that list one might also add guilt-ridden. The Good News of this "Divine Design of Harmony" between heaven and earth took relatively few years before it began to be re-styled. The changes that soon appeared produced a vision of a holiness that was unnatural in its striving to be supernatural. In this vision, the flesh (body) was evil, the earth was a moral battlefield in which creation was filled with hidden traps for those who sought to be one with the Divine Creator. Some Greek philosophers and early spiritual teachers taught that perfection was to be found in escaping from the earth, from the flesh and the world — the Ascension or Assumption Syndrome.

Today, we bear the wounds of hundreds of years of religious wars between the spirit and the flesh, instead of tasting the fruit of a communion between the two. Anyone who prays the ancient psalms of Israel knows how, for the composer, nature and God were interwoven. This divine union was expressed not simply in all the countless beauties of the earth and sea, but in the complex emotions and aspects of human nature as well. St. Francis of Assisi understood the Good News. He returned to a simplicity of nature, believing that all creation was part of the Body of Christ. He could call animals, birds and the elements of the earth by names like brother and sister. In so doing, he was following the spiritual Way of his Lord who also lovingly embraced nature. Were the Gospels to be written today, we might wonder how many of the events would take place outside. A good bet would be that 99% would happen inside (a house, building or a car) since that is where today we spend most of our time.

We do not feel at home with nature, or we often feel guilty about its powerful movements in our bodies, and because of this we will not easily embrace a natural spirituality. Because we delight in acts of manipulation or control of nature, we tend not to desire a more natural spirituality. But without a delight in the natural, we shall find it difficult to truly follow in the steps of our Lord.

A natural spirituality, moreover, would not be that difficult. It would simply be attempting to live our lives in a more "natural" way. Perhaps no other group in history has lived such unnatural lives as we

17

presently are attempting to do.

Some simple questions to examine our own spiritualities might be the following:

(a) Do our living environments and personal habits bring us into contact with creation or do they separate us from it? Do we find patterns for our behavior from machines (IBM efficiency, running day and night) or from nature? Do our virtues flow from nature or are they the result of a "war" against nature?

(b) Does the food we eat fill our bodies with energy and life or with junk? Do we seek natural foods or prefer artificial ones? Is meal time also communion time?

(c) How do we respond to rain, snow and dust? Do we run to get out of the rain or do we experience the wet marvel of this sister of creation? Are rain, sun and wind (hard on hairdos) and all kinds of weather experienced as times of communion or are they tolerated as times of inconvenience?

(d) Do our lives reflect the balanced rhythms of the earth? Do we live balanced lives of work and rest, study and play, prayer and leisure, or do we live lives overfilled with work and stressful living?

(e) Can we enter into the earthen worship of sunrise, sunset and noonshine? Do our lives allow us time to touch the earth and learn her mysteries? Is physical exercise part of our daily spirituality — walking, jogging, or whatever? We easily forget that part of our nature is to be "on the move" and we were not intended to spend entire days seated.

(f) Do we find God, the Holy, in the middle of our earthly lives and in the 10,000 corners of creation or do we find God by retreating from these? Can we believe that the next world is inside this one?

These are but a few, a very few, questions that may help us to look at our own spiritualities. Perhaps they may assist us in finding more of nature in our lives and more natural spiritualities.

But one may ask, "Won't all this involvement in earthy, material things only make us more materialistic than we already are?" That's the humor in the paradox, for we are not really materialistic at all, since we fail to find pleasure in matter. Rather, we are collectivistic, since we take more pleasure in collecting material things than in using them. For many people in a consumer society it is more fun to go shopping, more fun to buy things than to use them or wear them.

The real cosmic humor would be if by daily descending deeply into nature we would discover that we had actually discovered the Divine.

Canticle of Creation

In the beginning, Lord my God,
    You alone existed: eternally one
    yet pregnant in the fullness of unity.
Full to overflowing,
    You, Father of All Life, exploded outward
    in a billion bits and pieces.
Your Word became flesh,
    whirling in shining stars, shimmering suns
    and in genesis glimmering galaxies.
You, my God, spoke
    and Your Words became flesh:
    in sun and moon, earth and seas,
    mountains and gentle hills,
    rolling rivers and silent streams.
You, my God, spoke
    and Your Words became flesh:
    in winged bird, in deer and elephant,
    in grazing cow, racing horse, and fish of the deep.
Your Words, so unique and so varied,
    filled the earth also with rabbit, squirrel and ant.
And all Your Words were beautiful,
    and all were good.

From each of these Holy Words
    arose a prayer of praise and adoration
    to You, their Creator
    and Wondrous Womb.
"Praise You," rang out the redwood,
    "Blessed be You," chimed in the cedar,
    "Holy are You," prayed the prairie grasses.
From all four corners of this earth,
    rose up a chorus of perpetual adoration.

O Sacred Spirit, O Divine Breath of Life,
 unseal my ears that they may ever listen
 to Your continuous canticle of creation;
 open my heart and my whole self,
 to sing in harmony with all its many voices.
Teach me to commune with Your first Word made flesh,
 Your creation,
 that I may be able to unravel the wondrous words
 of Your second Word made flesh,
 Jesus,
 through whom, with whom, and in whom,
 I may see myself as another Word of Yours made flesh,
 to Your glory and honor.

Amen+

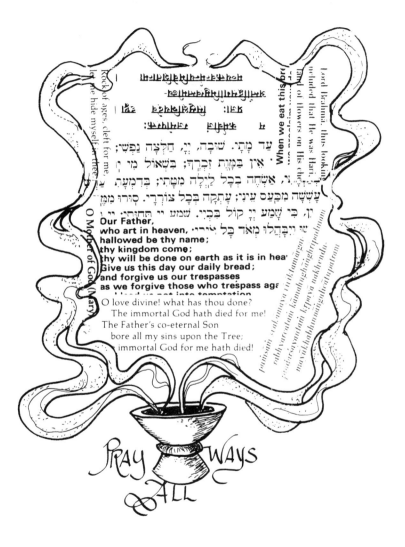

עַד מָתַי. שׁוּבָה, יְיָ, חַלְּצָה נַפְשִׁי;
אֵין בַּמָּוֶת זִכְרֶךָ; בִּשְׁאוֹל מִי יֹ
ג, אָשְׂחֶה בְכָל לַיְלָה מִטָּתִי; בְּדִמְעָת
עָשְׁשָׁה מִכַּעַס עֵינִי; עָתְקָה בְּכָל צוֹרְרָי. סוּרוּ מִמֶּ
יְיָ, כִּי שָׁמַע יְיָ קוֹל בִּכְיִי. שָׁמַע יְיָ תְּחִנָּתִי; יְיָ
שׁ יֵבֹשׁוּ וְיִבָּהֲלוּ מְאֹד כָּל יֵיִרִי.

Our Father,
who art in heaven,
hallowed be thy name;
thy kingdom come;
thy will be done on earth as it is in hea'
Give us this day our daily bread;
and forgive us our trespasses
as we forgive those who trespass aga
 I lead us not into temptation

O love divine! what has thou done?
  The immortal God hath died for me!
The Father's co-eternal Son
  bore all my sins upon the Tree;
  immortal God for me hath died!

Lord Brahma, thus looking

neluded that He was Hari;

and of flowers on His che

When we eat this bre

Rock of ages, cleft for me,
let me hide myself in thee.

O Mother of God (Mary

PRAY WAYS ALL

Praying with the Eyes

To pray is to involve the entire body in an act of communion with the Divine Mystery. Frequently we have thought about the art of prayer only as an activity of the intellect, "the raising of the mind to God." But we have been given two marvelous, though often overlooked, instruments of prayer: our eyes. We have only to open them in wonder to find that with them we can pray in many ways.

In the Gospels we are given an admonition concerning our prayer life: "Be constantly on the watch! Stay awake! It is like a man traveling abroad. He leaves home and places his servants in charge, each with his own task; and he orders the man at the gate to watch with a sharp eye" (Mk 13:33-34). We are charged to "look around," to have our eyes open and to be awake. This wide-eyed attitude of vigilance is an important part of a lifestyle of "praying always." Is it not a bit ironic that the invitation, "Let us pray . . . ," so often stimulates in us the physical response of closing our eyes? This reaction, often a combination of habit, custom and practicality, closes off the use of one of the vital organs of our body. Could we not, when invited to pray, cup our hands

23

over our ears instead?

Buildings are like persons; they also have eyes which we call windows. One function of windows is to allow us to look out at the world that surrounds our homes. Church buildings have eyes as well, but usually they are closed with stained glass eyelids. Places of prayer seem to shut out the surrounding environment with these beautiful eyelids by painting on them images of holy people and symbols. Why? Do we close our eyes when we pray for the same purpose, that is, to shut out distractions and sights that might take our minds away from God? Were we to hold the philosophy that the world is evil, then to shut out the world from prayer and from places of prayer would indeed make good sense. But is that what we believe as Christians: that creation, our environment, is a distraction from God?

This prayer habit of closing our eyes, when seen in relation to some of our other human activities, is indeed a curious religious custom. If, for example, prayer is understood as talking to God, should we not likewise close our eyes when we speak to one another? If we see prayer as communion with God, should we not also close our eyes when we wish to enter into communion with some event or some person? Rather, getting into the flow of a sporting event, a painting, or a conversation, with its moments of non-verbal communication, requires that we be more attentive than normal, that we take in more with our eyes.

God, of course, is beyond sight and chooses to express Himself in ways that are not available to the eyes alone. In the prayer of meditation, the prayer of centering, for example, we seek the mystery of the Divine Presence not outside of us in the marvelous world of creation but rather within us. We search within the depths of our hearts, carefully looking into the mystery of our unique personhood. In this type of prayer, in meditation, it is an aid to close the eye-shades of the windows of the body so that we can focus our attention upon the mystery within, so that we may listen to the hidden word expressing itself to us. This being understood, we are still confronted by the non-use of the gift of our eyes in our prayer lives.

Possibly, we close our eyes at times of prayer, such as at meal blessings, because the surrounding environment is so overwhelming. Persons blind from birth who, by intricate eye operations are given the gift of sight after years of non-sight, usually suffer from visual shock! In *Pilgrim at Tinker Creek,* Annie Dillard tells of a twenty-two year old woman who, through a delicate operation on her eyes, was able to see. The young woman was bedazzled by the world's brightness, a brilliance that you and I so take for granted that we fail to see its splendor. The shock was so great that she kept her eyes shut for two weeks after that first opening. Finally, with the encouragement of her doctor, she slowly began to open her eyes and to direct her gaze on what surrounded her. She exclaimed over and over again, "O God, O God . . . how beautiful, how beautiful!"

Look around you! Our eyes are key-holes opening to a wonder world. With these twin gifts we peek out at the Divine Mystery which surrounds us in everything and everyone. Our two eyes are so small that they account for less than one percent of the weight of the human head, yet oh how marvelous they are! Marvelous indeed, yet how little we value them as instruments of prayer and union with God!

The experience of the young woman who was stunned by the world's brilliance is similar to that of the 12th century saint, Hildegard. In a vision, Saint Hildegard saw a fair human form who spoke of its i-dentity in these words: "I am that supreme and fiery force that sends forth all the sparks of life. Death has no part in me, yet I do allow it. Wherefore I am girt with wisdom as with wings. I am that living and fiery essence of the Divine Substance that glows in the beauty of the fields. I shine in the water, I burn in the sun and the moon and the stars. Mine is that mysterious force of the invisible wind. I sustain the breath of all the living. I breathe in the grass and in the flowers, and when the waters flow like living things, it is I ... I am life!" Eyes are the prayer books of mystics, and each of us has been equipped with these wonderful mystic prayer instruments!

Having been told "Look around you ..." and having also been told "Pray always," perhaps we could combine these two charges and use our eyes as a means of perpetual adoration. How do we pray with our eyes? First, in those times of worship in which signs or symbols are used, let us pray by looking. Words that are spoken in ritual are intended only to support these primal, visual prayers. The visuals are so loaded with meaning that often the words of ritual only get in the way of what is a more immediate expression of prayer. At the celebration of Mass, for example, the lifting up of the bread, the breaking of the bread, a silver cloud of incense, the sacred cup of communion raised high above our heads — all these are looking-prayers. While praying at the Eucharistic tables of supper, lunch or dinner in our homes, we should look with awe and gratitude at the crisp green salad, the deep red of the tomato soup, the whiteness of clean plates and the crystal shine of water glasses. At times like these, to close our eyes to pray may not shut out distractions but, perhaps, may shut out God!

We need to learn how to let what we see change from distraction to devotion. Our friends in the Zen Buddhist tradition have something to share with us. When we speak of the Zen art of drinking tea, which began to flower shortly after a 12th century Zen Buddhist priest by the name of Eisai was the first to plant tea seeds in Japanese culture, we remember that Zen monks carried the art of tea-drinking into public life. This ceremony encourages reverence, peace and a sense of purposefulness in life. Attention and mindfulness are given to everything as a means of opening the third eye, the eye of the soul. One aspect of the tea ceremony is the inspection by the guests of the tea cups, spoons and other objects to be used. These are not viewed merely as practical necessities. Rather, to see — to really behold — these beautiful objects is an essential part of the total experience of the tea ceremony. The guests find the pleasure of wonder as they experience the beauty of all that is involved in the act of making and drinking tea.

Keeping this Zen custom in mind, let us look back to the 4th century in the ancient city of Jerusalem. There Saint Cyril, the bishop of Jerusalem, spoke about the Holy Eucharist: "When you approach Communion . . . make your left hand a throne for the right one, which is to receive the King . . . after having sanctified your eyes by contact with the Holy Body . . . ." This instruction on receiving Holy Communion in the hands is an interesting counsel on the use of our eyes, the making holy of our eyes by simply looking (or perhaps by looking simply). To truly enter into the renewal of the liturgy of Communion will mean much more than simply a change in ritual, a change from receiving Communion in the hands instead of on the tongue. Hopefully, this renewal will bring a greater awareness of how to live in Communion — to live with hands, feet, tongues, ears and eyes at prayer and in communion with God. We look with our eyes, touching with our vision the cup and the bread. First, we must be able to see the texture, the line, the color be-

27

fore we can move to that which is beneath the surface — to the inner beauty. From our Zen friends, we can borrow the custom of treating the instruments of the Mass with great and loving care, allowing our eyes to caress the altar, the cup, the plate . . . to be carried into the Divine Mystery by touching with our eyes the cloud of incense or the flame of the candle. And this prayerful treatment should extend beyond the liturgy of the Eucharist into each corner of our daily lives, so that we enter a communion of seeing the crusty brown bread of breakfast, the chunky, creamy soup of supper, for to really see is to make our eyes holy as well.

In this way our eyes can be of great value as instruments of communion and gratitude. We can use them to drink in the sights that meet our eyes and, in silence, to absorb the light that shines within them. We could take our time to truly look at someone we love, or at a tree or a sunset . . . not saying anything, but simply looking and beholding and so being in communion. We can also sharpen the focus of our visual wonder by adding to it a commentary of what we are seeing. It seems that if we call attention to what we are looking at, we see more and see more clearly. So, when we look out a window, we can say to ourselves: "Well, look at the grey trees with their tall bare branches reaching up into the blue skies, the brown dead leaves clinging to the limbs of the oak. A blue jay hopping along on the snow-covered earth." Try it the next time you take a walk or look out your window and see if you don't see more than you ever did before. And as you are seeing, realize that you are also praying — praying as a mystic!

And, the next time someone says, "Let us pray," you might also try opening your eyes and simply testing the result. As commonplace as what you see may seem, keep in mind the words of our Lord:

"Blessed are the eyes that see what you see, kings and prophets longed to see that, but did not . . ." (Lk 10: 23-24).

A Prayer of Gratitude
for the Gift of Sight

Creator God, Holy Parent, I give You thanks
    for all of Your so often unnoticed natural gifts.
I rejoice especially, now, in my eyes,
    these two tiny but marvelous gifts
    that add so much to the fullness of my life.
This gift of sight enlarges the world of my enjoyment
    and magnifies my appreciation of nature,
    of great works of art, of the gifts of books and print,
    of those persons I love —
    and for this I am grateful.

I thank You also for the gift of insight
    by which my spirit sees and understands.
For the gift of the third eye,
    the eye of the heart,
    by which I may stand-under the meaning of life,
    I am indeed grateful.

I am especially thankful for Your Son, Jesus,
    star-born prophet, whose very coming
    was a healing light to the world,
    who opened the eyes of the blind
    and gave to a weary world new sight.

29

Blessed be all those who have taught me to see:
prophets, poets, writers and movie-makers,
friends and lovers, all teachers of vision.

May my eyes bless You this day;
may they be opened-prayers of gratitude,
as I attempt to overcome any blindness of heart
and any dullness of appreciation of the wonder of sight.

In the fullness of my being,
I bless You, Incomprehensible Lord,
who foresees a heaven of such splendor,
that ear has not heard nor eye seen
such beauty as You have prepared.

Blessed are You, Lord my God,
for the wondrous gift of sight.

Amen+

The Prayer of Tears

Our eyes are not only the windows of the soul and organs of enjoyment, they are also the instruments of joy and sorrow. While we feel deeply the pain of departure or the intense experience of other emotions, these are not easily shown. Our eyes are sacraments for these beautiful and deeply felt feelings. Even our tears become a way for us to "pray all ways."

Tears and laughter are universal languages, for they are understood by people of every nation. Crying is part of our basic birth equipment and so is a gift from God. While its source is divine, crying is usually a source of embarrassment for us. Crying, while embarrassing, is also an honest and an incarnational or bodily prayer that reaches the ear and heart of God.

The spiritual master, Jesus, and His disciples, together with a large crowd, came one day to the city gates of Naim. As they approached the city, they met a funeral procession of a widow who was on her way to bury her only son. He was touched by the sorrow of the widow and saying, "Do not cry," He restored her son to life (Lk 7: 11-15). His heart was deeply touched and without any request from the mother,

He performed a wonder, a miracle. Her tears were her prayers and those prayers were heard. Tears are indeed powerful prayers, for they possess the power to move even heaven. Tears perform numerous functions, besides being the most powerful of all languages. Tears are able to express that which is beyond the power of words.

Tears also are necessary for health. Their biological function is to keep the eyes moist and clean. Tears constantly heal, protect and cleanse with their marvelous solution. When we cry, as did the widow from Naim, that special cleansing solution flows in great abundance. If it were not for the constant presence of tears in our eyes, we would suffer serious eye problems and even possibly the loss of sight. The inability to cry is a serious health problem, as well as a serious emotional problem.

We began this chapter with the observation that crying and laughing are universal languages. We may also add that tears are considered by many to be a woman's language! We realize, of course, that this is not true, but it is the way our society views crying. King Lear expressed this opinion in Shakespeare's famous play when he said, "Let not women's weapons, waterdrops, stain my man's cheeks!" It is "unseemly" for a man to cry in public. Women and children may cry in public, but not a man! That weeping is a sign of weakness is an attitude instilled in us in early childhood. Such an attitude is strange, since crying was the first form of communication we possessed. The cry of the infant is a message always heard by the parent. Babies are unable to laugh until they are about twenty weeks old, but they can cry with their first breath. A few years later, as children, we attempted to gain our parent's attention by use of that infant language. When we did so, we were told, "Stop acting like a baby and stop your crying this instant!" If we were boys, we were told,"Stop crying and be a man!" We all, men and women, learned that lesson and today attempt to control this natural if inappropriate behavior of crying.

Shakespeare, if he may be quoted again, hinted at another aspect that makes crying in public suspect. In *Taming of the Shrew,* he wrote," . . . a woman's gift to rain a shower of commanded tears." Since it is possible to "command" tears to appear when needed, we are naturally suspicious of the weeping-willow type who cries at the slightest sign of difficulties. But even if tears can be used illegitimately, it is wrong and psychologically dangerous to view them only as "a woman's language."

Tears are the prayer-beads of all of us, men and women, because they arise from a fullness of the heart. Such an overflowing of the heart can be the result of great sorrow, but also of great joy. Tears appear as we listen to a moving speech in a play, while viewing a motion picture, while taking part in a departure of a friend, or when absorbed in some deeply moving religious experience. All expressions of the heart are good prayer. What happens naturally is usually good and also right. When this experience comes to us, we should not listen to the inner voice that condemns crying or attempts to make us feel shame for tears. We do not ask to be excused when we laugh, why should we when we cry? We don't attempt to suppress laughter, why should we attempt to "shut off" our tears? While, according to most customs, it is inappropriate to laugh in church, we can wonder, "Is it also inappropriate to cry in worship?" Perhaps we should explore more ways to laugh and cry as we worship God, or at least to allow more room for these expressions when they arise naturally. If tears are good prayer, it would be a shame to forbid them in the times of prayer.

Why is crying good prayer? Crying can be good prayer for several reasons, but one is that when we cry we are "out of control." Most prayer is well manicured, like the local country club lawn, organized if not memorized, read if not dead. Most prayer begins with the same words and ends with the same words, all very controlled and well managed. But crying is not controlled; rather it is free and flowing — springing up from the inside, from the heart and not the head.

We usually fear what we are unable to control. What we are not in control of is dangerous and therefore bad! Crying and laughing are usually not part of the image of the saint, the religious ideal, because they manifest a lack of control. If one is to be holy, then nature must be controlled and not allowed free room to play, at least so we are told. The mind loves to be in charge of the heart. When an attack of non-control hits, as when we begin to weep, the mind is busy turning knobs and dials to get back in control again.

Tears are an expression of lack of control. They are prayer because prayer is communion with that which is beyond our control: God. A reporter was once interviewing an Indian guru about his work in giving spiritual instruction to Americans. The reporter asked the spiritual master, "What is the first thing you attempt to teach Americans?" The old man replied, "I try to teach them how to cry again."

Tears are sacraments of humility, for when we are controlling things, events and people, we easily forget our creaturehood and slip easily into thinking we are gods. True prayer is a paradox, for while embracing the creaturehood of our humanity, we are also encircled in the unifying mystery of the oneness of God and all creation.

When in our daily lives events touch us deeply

and we begin to feel that growing fullness that is the overture of tears, we can let go and flow with the Prayer of the Heart instead of fighting for control. Not attempting to speak or even to form appropriate words, we can simply pray the Prayer of Tears. We can pray the prayer of tearful gratitude or defeat, the prayer of tearful departure or misunderstanding. The prayerbook of tears is full of beautiful prayers — the psalms of theater, poetry and music, and canticles of great movements and frustration. As we pray these prayers we can resist any temptation to be "tough" or "rigid" and instead be relaxed and fully human.

Also, when others are tearful, we can relax and be comfortable with them. For the person who is not crying and is with one who is, tears are a source of distress. Usually we attempt to help the crying person stop because it will make *us* feel better! As the distressful situation is removed we feel relieved. Crying at a funeral is natural and is socially expected, but crying at other times causes shame, embarrassment and guilt by those who witness it. But if we could view our tears as prayers, the next time we are with persons who are crying, we can let them cry as long and as hard as they wish and join them by our silent but supportive presence. Viewing our tears as prayerful activity, we would perhaps see them as they truly are — a valuable expression of mature people, human and also divine.

Divine? Yes, for in Jesus we find a pattern for our prayer and our lifestyles. He prayed the Prayer of Tears over the city of Jerusalem, at the tomb of His good friend, Lazarus, and probably at numerous other times not recorded for us. Perhaps He cried with joy as a friend and neighbor were married at Cana. Perhaps tears ran down His face as He was overcome, out of control with emotion, as He celebrated that mystical meal with His friends the night before He died.   37

To the Greek and Roman mind, such behavior on the part of a divine person was unthinkable! God is beyond emotion; God is beyond being moved by some human event or need. To be touched or "moved" by tears was to be in the control of another and therefore to be a non-God. The beautiful story of Naim tells us that not only was Jesus moved but He was moved to make a miracle. In the person of Jesus we see the compassion, the love and the reality of the Godhead. The good news of the Gospel is that we are loved by such a divine person.

This aspect of the divine-parent God is shown in an old rabbinical tale about Moses and the chosen children. The crossing of the Red Sea by Moses was watched by all the citizens of heaven, angels and saints. As Moses raised his staff after they crossed the sea and the waters came crashing back again destroying all the Egyptian army, horses and chariots, a great shout arose in heaven. Everyone was full of joy. One of the angels looked over at the throne of God, only to see that God was crying. Large tears were silently streaming down the divine face. The angel said, "Blessed are You, All Holy and Divine Lord of Hosts, why are You crying? Your chosen children are safe; they are victorious!" God, wiping the tears from His cheeks said, "Yes, I know . . . but you see, the Egyptians are My children as well!"

God hears the prayers that flow from our hearts. Laughter and tears reach heaven with the speed of laser beams. As our crying was heard by our parents when we were infants, so our tears today are heard by the Divine Parent.

When we have learned to cry without shame, allowing our hearts to speak that most ancient and universal of all tongues, we will know that we are truly mature people, truly human and also, so it seems, divine as well!

The Prayer of Tears

Lord, Beloved God,
    since all communion with You is prayer,
    may even my tears be psalms of petition
    and canticles of praise to You.
This is a prayer that You value greatly:
    the prayer of my tears;
    it is a prayer that You always hear
    for You are a compassionate and kind God.
And, Lord, I know You understand
    that when I am overcome by my tears —
    unable to speak or form a prayer —
    that these very tears voice volumes of verse.

All truly great prayer
    rises from deep inside
    and springs spontaneously to the surface.
It would then seem
    that from among the many beautiful prayers,
    the sacred songs and canticles of praise,
    my tears may be the best worship of all.

Help me not to be ashamed of them;
    show me how I can let go of control
    and let this prayer of my heart, my tears,
    flow naturally and freely to You,
    my Blessed Lord and Divine Lover.
In times of joy or sorrow,
    blessed be my tears,
    the holy prayers of my heart.

Amen+

Praying
Through the Nose

Paying, not praying, through the nose is a familiar expression. It seems that when a census was taken in ancient times, people were counted by the act of counting noses. A relic of this remains in our expression, "Let's count noses to see how many are here." Paying through the nose is an expression that arose from the poll tax that followed the census. In Sweden, this tax that followed the census was called a Nose Tax.

While we easily forget our noses, we are made aware of them when we suffer from the sniffles, from hay fever or a common cold. But dripping or not, the nose is a bodily organ we use all the time. It is also a marvelous organ of prayer. Smelling as prayer, while sounding rather bizarre, should be "as plain as the nose on your face."

In fact, according to Sacred Scripture, it all began with the nose: "The Lord God formed man out of the clay of the ground and blew into his nostrils the breath of life and so man became a living being." The writer of Genesis tells us that humanity's spiritual creation was achieved through the nose. Not surprising then that the philosopher Gustav Jager insisted that a person's soul lies in his smells. Yet, for most of us, nothing seems so remote from our worship and prayer as our noses. The reasons why we have failed to develop this art and prayer of smelling could be numerous, some of which will be considered later in this reflection. It is strange that while we use our eyes, ears, hands and the rest of our bodies in worship, our noses are often forgotten aids on our way to heaven.

Although we have forgotten our noses, the ancient ones thought it was important not to forget God's nose. Noah, after the great flood, came forth from the ark and built an altar. Choosing victims from among the animal passengers of his ark, he offered a holocaust, a burnt sacrifice to the Lord God. We are told in the same book of Genesis that "When the Lord smelled the sweet odor, He said to Himself, 'Never again will I doom the earth . . .'" (Gen 8:21). From that time onward, people were anxious to please God with fragrant-smelling sacrifices and prayers that "rose upward like incense." The use of incense among ancients was both as a sacrifice and as an aid to prayer. The use of incense is world-wide, found among many religions and peoples. When its aroma arises, the nose prays and also, it seems, God's nose is delighted. Incense gives that special whiff to worship; it is the smell of prayer and adoration.

We are told that we have stored within our brain a catalog of 50,000 different smells. The smell of incense awakens the primitive memories of sacrifices and holocausts. These scent-memories are deeply buried in our DNA codes. For Catholics, Roman and Anglican, such savory memories are closer to the surface. The smell of incense triggers flashbacks to High Mass and Benediction, to Sacred Burials and a more mystical relationship with the Divine Mystery.

42

The old-timers say that an itchy nose is a sign that you will meet a stranger or that soon you will kiss a fool. Incense gives us an itchy nose to return to those precious moments of a more transcendental prayer when we sensed, if not smelled, a God who was beyond words and theological explanations. In the religions of the Western industrialized world, incense is an antique or an alien visitor from some exotic, Oriental religion. But we don't have to be a Zen disciple or a "super-orthodox traditionalist" to enjoy the pungent smell of incense or to use it as part of our prayer.

Incense is not restricted to temples or cathedrals. The use of incense in our personal prayer or in the family prayer of the home could add much to our devotion, if not also to our enjoyment of worship. Indeed, Eastern religions make much use of incense, but we should remember that Christianity appeared in the Near East, which is also the Near West. Incense with its delightful aroma is a global, catholic (small "c") prayer for the nose and a prayer for the eyes as the smoke slowly and gracefully ascends. Some caution is needed in its use, however. I know a young doctor and his wife who pray in their apartment and frequently use incense as part of their contemplative prayer. One time, he told me, he was a bit lavish with the spoonfuls of incense that he placed on the charcoal. Great, beautiful clouds of frankincense filled the apartment and then the hallway of the complex. The smoke of the incense set off the smoke detector and alarms began to ring ... ah, yes, moderation in all things! But the ancient and ever-youthful prayer of incense is but one way of worshipping with our noses. Remember, we also have 49,999 other smells with which to pray.

We can be forgiven for forgetting to pray with our noses because we are often overly concerned about their shapes or mis-shapes. The nose, which is located in the very center of the face, is important to the good looks or beauty of the person. With an eternal design, we were each given a special nose that was intended to fit a unique face. Whatever its shape, we should rejoice in that nose. Keep in mind that such a classic beauty as the famous Venus de Milo has a nose which is at least seven millimeters off center to the left! Physical beauty and love are related. Our nose is a part of our equipment for making love, perhaps more important than we realize. Dr. William Fliess, a friend of Freud's, considered the nose as the most important sexual organ! Those readers with large noses take note of such a theory. Recent experiments confirm that animals, including humans, are affected strongly by the different scents that come from the body. Human fragrance has had a part to play in our evolution and in the ancient history and mystery of mating. We know that Eskimos, Laplanders and even some peoples of the South Pacific Islands rub noses as a sign of affection instead of kissing. Since love and noses are interrelated, we may have a clue to a reason why we find ourselves strangers to the prayer of smelling.

Examine the books of the Bible and you will find an occasional mention of smelling. But in one book, The Song of Songs, there are numerous references to the delights of human fragrance. This part of the Sacred Scriptures has caused some unsavory scholarship. Both among the rabbinical and Christian scholars, the Song of Songs seemed almost too sensual, too erotic to be part of sacred writing. Pious solutions were sought; perhaps it was a parable, a story of some mystical relationship between God and Israel, between Christ and the Church. It was impossible to consider, until recent times, that it might be not a parable but a song of praise for human love

44

which was one of the numerous gifts given to us by a generous God. Religion throughout history has struggled to reconcile the sensual aspects of creation with a spiritual God and has usually concluded by rejecting the sensual and insisting on the "spiritual." Perhaps that is why we might not think about praying with our noses — and their pungent 50,000 perfumed prayers. But let us not too quickly condemn religion as the sole guilty party if we are a nose-less people. In Psalm 113 the psalmist speaks of the idols of the gods, but maybe he is really speaking of you and me: "They have eyes but they cannot see, they have ears but they cannot hear, they have nostrils but they cannot smell." While the pious and puritanical may indeed "turn up their noses" at the very thought of sensuality and spirituality being closely related, it is not that upward direction of the nose that is the sole cause of the problem. The problem may also be found in their being turned downward. Our noses are turned downward, pressed against the grindstone. "Keep your nose to the grindstone" is a proverb of Ole England meant to inspire industrious behavior. We may miss the "smell" of God and the other mystical delights of creation because all we can smell is the "grind." The smell that clogs our noses is that of the daily grind — its problems, tensions, the ever-increasing lack of free time, the constant rush of commitments. The smell of the grind may be the smell of success, but it is seldom the fragrance of love or prayer.

Recent studies have shown that as any culture becomes industrialized, it begins to have a great disdain for smells and odors, human and otherwise. Interesting! Perhaps such an attitude is a reaction to the offensive odors of pollution that accompany factories and machines. But maybe it arises from another source. What if the 50,000 different sniffs of life

45

might distract men and women from the work-work-work of the assembly line? Perhaps the high priests of capitalism are busy fumigating the fun out of life so we will all keep our noses to the grindstone. Look at the shelves of your supermarket. They are loaded with various sprays, powders, aerosols, and bottles of disinfectants that remove as many as possible of those thousands of natural smells of life. We are left with homes and bodies deodorized of the natural. Instead, our lives now smell sterile, artificial and chemically vacant. And so, undistracted by the powerful scents of life, we have more time to keep working harder and harder. While we are successful with our noses glued to the grindstone, we do miss the smell, taste, touch and sound of "Life," which happens to be God's middle name.

The famous entertainer, Eddie Cantor, told a story about himself. As a young man he worked hard and long to be a star. His grandmother told him one day, "Eddie, don't go so fast or you will miss the scenery." But instead of listening to his wise grandmother, he continued the race to stardom. One night at the opening of a smash success show and after the final curtain when a large crowd of admirers surrounded him, he received a telegram. It was from his wife, Ida. The telegram told him that their fourth daughter had just been born. There, backstage, in the midst of all the excitement and the echoes of the applause, he remembered the words of his grandmother, "You'll miss the scenery, Eddie." From that moment he said that he always took time to pause and take in the scenery of life. He took time for what was truly important instead of what was merely necessary for success.

You and I can easily miss the scenery of our lives when our noses are pressed, day and night, against the grindstone. We can also miss the "smell" of the

46

scenery, the aromatic pleasure that our creator-artist God designed to be an integral part of our sensual-spiritual way to heaven. The less sophisticated people of the world enjoy daily such aromatic pleasures, while we are unaware that they even exist. As time becomes more precious and a shortage of it increases, we will tend to rush all the more. Yet, we each have 168 hours of time every week and as Alec Mackenzie says, "No one has enough time, yet everyone has all there is!" What can we do, you might ask, if we wish to awaken our sleeping noses and learn how to pray with them? Will it be difficult to arouse our abilities to once again experience the aromatic? It will be easy if we are willing to take the time.

First, let us take time each day to smell. Take time to deeply inhale the fragrance of the early morning air or the smell of fresh rain. Take time to pause to enjoy the aroma of freshly brewed coffee.

Secondly, let us take time to unlock our culturally clogged noses so as to experience the natural fragrance of flowers, our lawns, trees and the earth itself. We might wonder how many of the 50,000 smells of life we encounter each day but are totally unaware that we have encountered them.

Thirdly, let us pause before each meal in order to bless our food with our noses. Every food and drink has its unique smell and unique bouquet, as we say of wine. The smell of food is not only pleasing, it also unlocks memories. It is said that if you wish to sell your house, bake a few loaves of bread before the prospective buyer arrives. The aroma of freshly baked bread will cause the memories of "home" and family to rush to the surface. Your prospective home buyer will be so moved that he or she will fail to see the cracks in the walls or the holes in the roof.

Fourthly, take time to externalize the pleasures that come to you through the sense of smell. Among the traditional prayers of gratitude of the Jewish spirituality are prayers like, "Blessed are You, Lord our God, who delights us with the fragrance of fruit trees." These and other mini-prayers express delight in the countless pleasures of the nose. Either externally or internally, we should take time to thank God for the treasure of a thousand tantalizing aromas.

Finally, when it comes time for formal prayer, we can take time to simply sit and watch our breathing . . . take the time to focus our attention on the miracle of breathing as life passes in and out of our nostrils. The Hopi Indians of the American Southwest express it simply and directly: "Breathing is praying." To pray such a prayer of the nose for ten minutes is to worship in the spirit of the Garden of Eden where God, the creator-lover, placed His mouth close to Adam's nose and performed a transcendental transplant — history's first transfusion. We can also add to this time of quiet sitting the presence of incense (caution for the smoke detectors). Perhaps its use will alert us to the natural incense of worship that rises continuously from everything in creation.

You and I have our personal, unique body-scent, as distinctive as our fingerprints. That body-scent is the unique, personal odor that makes it easy for bloodhounds to track us down. Who knows, perhaps God also has such a distinctive odor. God's scent is one, however, that is composed of all the 50,000 different smells of life, a Sacred Symphony of Smells. In conclusion to these suggestions of possible ways to pray with your nose, regardless if it is Roman, Greek, long, short, or pug, I might share one simple bit of advice:

If you are wondering which is the correct way to heaven, I would answer your question by quoting a common folk expression: "Don't worry; you can't miss it; it is straight ahead. Just follow your nose."

A Prayer of Gratitude
for the Gift of a Nose

Blessed are You, Lord of All Gifts,
  for Your masterful handiwork: the nose.
I thank You for the gift of my nose
  and its marvelous power of smelling life.
I rejoice in the sense of smell
  which brings delight to my meals,
  enhances the beauty of flowers
  and heightens the pleasure of love.

Show to me, Lord,
  how my nose can be a source of my prayer
  as I awaken to, sense and enjoy
  the ten thousand different incenses
  that arise from all things in praise of You,
  their holy and artistic Creator.

Regardless of the shape or size of the nose
  that You, my Creator, have given me,
  may it be for me an instrument of worship.
The next time I have the opportunity
  to meet an odor, a pleasant aroma or scent,
  make me aware that I am at prayer.
Allow me the grace to take each scent in,
  to relish it and to rejoice
  that You have made the possibility of prayer
  so easy and entertaining.

Blessed are You, Lord of Noses,
  for countless and varied smells.

Amen+

May
My
Prayer
Rise
Like
Incense
before
You

How to Pray
with Our Feet

As a form of prayer, the pilgrimage is an incarnational prayer, a prayer of the body. A pilgrim is a person who prays with the feet. In our present time, when greater and greater attention is being focused upon experiencing the Divine, the pilgrimage offers a form of prayer that can truly be experienced and lived. Christ Himself was often a pilgrim, traveling from His native Galilee to the Temple in Jerusalem for the ancient festivals. Even as a youth He took part in this religious expression. The Gospel story of the child Jesus being found in the Temple records one of these early pilgrimage experiences (Lk 2:41-52).

The prayer of the feet, the pilgrimage, is one of the most ancient and universal of prayers; it is prayer for the Christian, Moslem, Buddhist, Hindu and Jew. Part of the religious duties of a devout Moslem is the pilgrimage to Mecca. For Hindus, the holy journey leads to the river Ganges where one's sins are bathed away or it may involve climbing high into the Himalayan Mountains to find the source of the holy Ganges. Buddhists may pilgrimage to Sarnath in North India where the Buddha preached his first sermon. The Western Wall, the Wailing Wall of the

Temple in Jerusalem, is the sacred destination of Jews coming to Israel. For the Christian, it is the city of Rome and St. Peter's, Jerusalem and the Holy Land, and shrines such as those at Lourdes, Fatima and Guadalupe that call the pilgrim from his or her home.

The destinations of a sacred journey are as varied as the great variety of religions: a wall, a tomb, a mountain, a river, a wall, a rock, a church . . . . While pilgrimages may lead to a variety of places and of objects, each points to the same mystery: the Holy! The shrines that are the final end of the journey seem to radiate a special type of energy which we have in the past called grace. Regardless of what name we give to this power, its reality is felt today by millions all over this earth. Part of the reason for taking a pilgrimage is to take in some of this energy or grace, for centuries of history seem to verify that those who visit holy places come away radiating the energy-grace of those shrines. Further, physical, emotional and spiritual cures and cleansings have been and still are associated with many pilgrim shrines.

In America, a young country, we seem to lack those famous sacred mountains, rivers and places to which we might pilgrimage. Indeed, we have shrines, but they seem to be mostly political: Valley Forge, the Alamo, the Lincoln Memorial, buildings and places connected with our revolution and history. The great religious shrines, on the other hand, are at a great distance — across oceans. Is it possible to pray with our feet, to have the vocation of pilgrim, while remaining at home? In England during the Middle Ages, there was a great shrine to our Lady at Walsingham. The people believed that the stars of the Milky Way pointed a path to the shrine, and there is a poem that says:

> O stars that point to Walsingham,
> O roads that lead to Rome,

what can you offer a gypsy heart
that's forced to stay at home?

We might well ask the stars what they have to offer to those who stay at home with family and job, to those who cannot make a pilgrimage to Rome or Jerusalem. What is possible is a rocking-chair pilgrimage. The rocking-chair is that unique invention, particularly well-suited to Americans, that allows a person to be on the move while sitting still. A rocking-chair pilgrim is a person who can make a holy journey while staying at home. This is not merely a concession to practicality, for the vocation to be a pilgrim involves primarily an "interior footwork." Every Christian is called to be a pilgrim, a traveler who realizes that the journey takes him or her through this life to the Father.

We rocking-chair pilgrims may, however, want from time to time to make a short pilgrimage — not only as a means of communion with a world on pilgrimage but also as a reminder of our inner vocation and as a means of prayer. Toward what holy place shall we set our feet? As we begin to look closer, we can see that it is not necessary to cross oceans or journey through deserts, for there are shrines of the Holy close at hand. One of the more beautiful aspects of the pilgrimage is that the "new" is not always the best and that the "old" is not always useless and unexciting. For the pilgrimage is always directed toward some historical place where humanity has met the Divine Mystery. Could we not begin our pilgrimage by journeying to the place of our birth or that of our parents or grandparents; or to the tomb of the family dead? Our personal heritage is holy . . . for God has touched our lives perhaps most strongly at these places and at the special times of birth, marriage and death. In a society that tends to forget its connection with the past because of its present mobility, such a family pilgrimage could give a sense of direction and meaning to our lives. We could pilgrimage to the grave of a former teacher, priest, or friend who was truth and light to us. In almost every home, there is the family saint or holy-person who, while never listed in the official ranks of the Church's canonized, has been a true source of light to us. The rocking-chair pilgrimage could take us to a holy-place as close as the parish church, but what is important is not so much the where as the *how* of our pilgrimage. Whether we journey to Mecca or around the block, we should journey in the spirit of the ancient pilgrim. We close the door to our home, the door to that which is familiar — to all our possessions and goods — we say good-bye to family and friends and walk away with the idea that we may never return . . . as we place ourselves in the hands of God. The purpose of all trips, as G.K. Chesterton used to say, is to come home. So, the purpose of the pilgrimage is to come home — but to come home with new eyes and a new heart. If we return home the same as when we left, then the pilgrimage has not been successful and perhaps has just been a pious vacation where shrines are visited instead of nightclubs.

The same vocation exists for those who stay home and make a pilgrimage and for those who travel abroad. The rules for pilgrimages hold true not only for the time our feet are on the road but for our whole life-journey. The first rule for the pilgrim is to travel simply. The pilgrimage should help in discerning that which is essential in our lives and that which is not. We should take with us only those possessions we really need, and experience teaches us what sort of possessions tend to become a burden: those things we are forced to carry only to protect. The journey can help us to learn how to live more simply and single-mindedly — what things to value and what things to regard lightly.

Secondly, the pilgrim leaves home, saying good-bye to loved ones and to the familiar, to travel to the unfamiliar, the unknown. This is never easy since we fear the unknown and tend to surround ourselves with all sorts of things that tell us that we are not really far from home, whether it be the local radio station if that be within range or, if overseas, American hotels and foods. Yet this journey into the unknown can be the very cause of our placing our trust in God. And if the journey is only a short distance from home, we can travel in the spirit of seeing the familiar as the unknown — which it essentially is because of existing within the Divine Mystery. In leaving behind the familiar, the pilgrim often travels alone and yet travels with others who are bound for the same shrine. Each pilgrim, whether on the way to Rome or the Holy Land or on the larger road of following Christ as the "Way," shares the road with others, and we find in the course of our life that this is the royal way.

Thirdly, by its very nature, since it is a journey away from the familiar toward the unfamiliar, the pilgrimage is an adventure. Yet the pilgrim must be on guard lest the adventure of the pilgrimage steal his attention away from the "inner-venture," the inner journey of the Spirit that every person in this world is making toward God. Thus it is necessary that the goals of the journey be always kept in mind so that the temptation to turn the vocation of a pilgrim into the vacation of the pilgrim is realistically faced. A good pilgrimage allows time for prayerful attention — to be aware of the movements of the "inner-venture."

Fourthly, though serious about the intention of the journey, the Christian pilgrim knows that joy is also part of the pilgrimage. We should enjoy our journey, as we should enjoy life, God and holiness.

Often we find the "grim" aspect of the pilgrimage in a sentimentally religious attitude that mistakes showy piousness for the holy! The Christian pilgrim is reverent, but this does not imply being downcast and grim, but rather being filled with a sense of awe, wonder and a childlike interest in all that is met on the journey.

This childlike awe brings us to the next point: that we are to travel with a new set of eyes and ears. For the pilgrim is a person who sees and hears differently than one who lives at home. The pilgrim takes nothing for granted, explores each person, place and thing; open to the hand of God, the voice of God, the face of God in all that is met on the holy road. Therefore, the fifth rule of the road suggests that we arrange our journey so that we have time to see, smell, taste and feel; time to be one with all that we encounter. This is necessary so that our prayer of the feet be not only incarnational — one of the body — but also contemplative, the type of prayer where we are able to become one with the holy-place rather than simply walk around it. Contemplation is a way of getting lost on the pilgrimage: lost in the beauties, the wonders and the mystery of the shrines. While on pilgrimage several years ago, I met an old holy man in northern India who said to me: "You are the most unusual American pilgrim I have ever met. You do not have a camera or a wristwatch." Since we are in a hurry, not only on the pilgrimage but in life as well, we have no time to get lost, to absorb the things around us. The ever-present shortage of time, the long list of places we wish to visit and things we wish to do, all make it necessary for us to rush about, our cameras clicking, while we say to ourselves: "When I get home I will sit down with these photos and really enjoy this place!" The truly wise pilgrim knows that the sacred cannot be captured on film but only invited into the heart. If we wish to bring back the "holy" from the holy-place, then we must bring an open, "exposable" heart rather than just a camera.

Sixthly, the pilgrim is historically a person who has had to face danger. This has always been part of the tradition of the road . . . the holy road to Rome or Jerusalem. The pilgrim has had to be prepared to face thieves, highwaymen, bandits and even death. Besides these, there have always been storms, plagues and pirates on the high seas — not to mention the danger from one's fellow pilgrims. At one time, in ancient days, Irish monasteries had the custom of sending monks on pilgrimage for the slightest infraction of the Holy Rule. It was also the custom of civil authorities to send criminals on pilgrimage to make restitution for their crimes. These two groups often met and traveled together, as is the custom of pilgrims, much to the injury of monastic vocations. But the dangers of any pilgrimage should not frighten away the potential pilgrim, for the danger is part of the prayer. Modern pilgrims must face revolution, hijacking, war and sickness — not to mention peddlers and souvenir hawkers. The ideal pilgrimage is one that includes a profound trust: the incarnational expression that the Lord is indeed our shepherd and guide and that our reliance is on Him and not merely in our own personal defenses. Away from home, no longer protected by normal support systems, we can experience the love and concern of God for us in a radically new way as we journey to the holy-place. At the heart of the prayer of the pilgrimage is experiencing the overwhelming providence of the Father.

Existing within the life of the Spirit is a universal call to pilgrimage, to the prayer of the feet. If we feel that since we cannot leave Burlington, Iowa or Poughkeepsie, New York — or whatever our home town — that this invitation does not apply to us, then we will have missed the opportunity for many graces. Every person who has read this can be and should be a pilgrim. In this era when greater and greater emphasis is being placed on prayer, those who fail to respond to the call of the "holy road" also fail to experience one of the most beautiful and ancient of prayers. We are called to be pilgrims, for that is what we really are anyway; all our life is but a journey to the Holy, whom we call God. It is a journey to be made in holy simplicity, and each pilgrimage is but a dress rehearsal for our own death when we shall close the door of our life upon our loved ones, family and possessions, and leave in *total* poverty on that journey to our Father. We are indeed pilgrims by birth; as J.D. Salinger has said: "All we do our whole lives is go from one little piece of holy ground to another."

A Blessing Prayer for a Journey

Blessed are You, Lord, my God,
    for You have created a wide and wonderful world
    in which I may travel.
Be my ever-near companion, O Holy Guide of Travelers,
    each time that I journey,
    and spread the road before me
    with beauty and adventure.
May all the highways ahead of me
    be free of harm and evil.

May I be accompanied by Your holy spirits,
    Your angelic messengers,
    as were the holy ones of days past.

On each trip may I take with me,
    as part of my traveling equipment,
    a heart wrapped in wonder with which to rejoice
    in all that I shall meet.

Along with the clothing of wonder,
    may I have room in my luggage
    for a mystic map
    by which I can find the invisible meanings
    of the events of this journey —
    of possible disappointments and delays,
    of possible breakdowns and rainy day troubles.
Always awake to Your sacred presence,
    to Your divine compassionate love,
    may I see in all that happens to me,
    in the beautiful and the bad,
    the mystery of Your holy plan.

May the blessing of God, the Father, Son and Holy Spirit,
    be upon me whenever I venture out on a journey
    and bring me home again in safety and peace.

Amen+

Play as Prayer

As children, we grew up with one truth deeply implanted in our subconscious: "Don't play in church!" Play and prayer, play and the worship of God, were not considered to be compatible. Perhaps as a result of that early training, we find it difficult if not impossible to pray as we play. Yet, we will not be able to pray in all ways until we are able to feel comfortable playing around with God. At first reading, this sounds foolish — and it is. We all have to learn how to be comfortable with being fools if we are to be disciples of the Holy Fool, Christ.

As children, play came naturally; it is an art-form that we, as adults, must re-learn. We are better workers than we are players. There may be historical reasons for this addiction to work. Professor Leakey, in the early 1960's, discovered the remains of a prehistoric person whom he named "Homo Habilis." This prehistoric person was so named because with the human remains were found the most ancient form of tools, hence the term "Habilis," which means "skillful." These early tools can be dated back almost 1,750,000 years. We have been working a long time, and we have come a long way from a tool made from a piece of chiseled animal bone or some rock strapped to a stick to our modern technology. We have in these thousands of years, almost 1¾ million years, moved from tools being the servants of workers to workers becoming the servants of their technological tools.

Can we now learn how "not-to-work" after all these thousands of centuries of learning "how-to-work?" Non-labor is leisure or play. Play is a term intentionally used since for many of us, recreation is hard work. We work at our occupations; we work at praying; we even work hard at having a good time. Play implies an absence of work and effort. Play is the main activity of children, however, and adults usually have problems with playing. We play golf or some musical instrument, but we do so for the sake of profit. A variety of such useful reasons such as recreation, health or entertainment helps us as adults to play without guilt. Pure play has no profit-value. Play is a human function and is not restricted to children. But to play we will have to learn how to stop working.

The eight-hour day for which workers fought in the late 1880's is a reality, and perhaps in our lifetime a four-day work week will be commonplace. But can we, even now, deal with our free time in a creative and playful way? When the workday ends, do we relax or are we so keyed up that we just continue working hard on non-occupational tasks? Each day we become increasingly busier. Even on our one "official" rest day, Sunday, we are rushing around, working hard at our leisure activities. Work is a habit and not necessarily a good one.

The sabbath, Jesus said, was made for us and not we for the sabbath. The holy day of non-work was to be a time to serve the needs of the human spirit which require more than work. Holy days were but "extra" sabbaths sprinkled throughout the year. They were times of play, feasting, dancing and communal celebration (Mardi Gras, Mid-Summer's Eve, All Saints). We might do well to recall these old feasts of fun. Adults and even youth in our technological, sophisticated society have forgotten how to truly celebrate. Murphy's law of evolution is in effect: "If you don't use it, you lose it." Sophistication prevents the child within from being playful, spontaneous and natural.

To those of our present generation, so ingrained into the values of hard work and its material rewards, it will be difficult to understand why people might have wanted to dance on a hilltop under the full moon or around a Mid-Summer's Eve bonfire if they didn't expect to get something out of it. Leisure or play has no value beyond itself. Free time, non-work time, should allow us the opportunities to play around with those things that cannot be priced or measured. Yet celebration and play are not without their rewards. On Christmas or any festival, we find ourselves lost in the midst of celebrating. We discover ourselves "belonging" to our ancient histories, to other people, and to that greater family of all, humanity. Fun — old-fashioned fun — is one of the fruits of leisure and playtime. Fun is always a gift to be shared with others. In fact, fun causes community to explode spontaneously. All of us are hungry for that sense of belonging and sharing. Deep down inside we know that life is meant to be more than work and continuous struggle. And whenever we celebrate together, we find that our burden of loneliness is lightened. No one can celebrate alone. Holidays and holy days by their very nature demand that they be shared. Sabbaths and shindigs are the means by which we keep ourselves human and holy.

God did not intend that we should live lives of

continuous, laborious struggle. Adam worked in the garden before the Fall. Who knows, perhaps the Fall injured the balance of the child and the adult in our first parents, and that congenital imbalance was passed on to us. We each have to learn how to regain our balance again. For God did not intend life to be some problem that we must untangle, but rather a dance to which we tango. Life is a balanced dance composed of work and play, of fast days and feast days, of times alone and times shared — a blend of the new and ancient.

We will learn this wholesome, healthy and holy dance if we can learn how to play again. We must practice laying aside our tools, so we can take up the art of play. We must take prayerful time to examine our tools carefully to see if they are our servants or if we are their servants.

As hard-working, stressful, busy, tired and overly adult people, we petition our Lord not to teach us how to pray, but . . . "Lord, teach us how to play." Those who playfully pray and prayerfully play will, at times, seem foolish to their neighbors, even to themselves. This role of the clown or fool that was once an accepted part of Christianity has recently fallen upon evil days. A feast day set aside for play and foolishness began long ago and is not the exclusive celebration of one religion. A feast of fools, since it touches the heart of the spiritual journey, belongs to the human family and to the cosmic temple of creation. Before the appearance of Christianity and organized religion, the ancient peoples of the earth celebrated a springtime feast of foolishness, a feast of the eternal child at play. It came at the beginning of spring as a way of thumbing one's nose at Old Man Winter and also at the Angel of Death. In the Middle Ages this holiday was a great favorite. Together with the pre-Christian feasts of Purim and Passover, April

64

Fools' Day and Easter were once part of a total celebration that winter was dead and that spring and life had been victorious.

Today's manner of keeping April Fools' Day is mild and tame, so tame that the ancients would never have even called it a celebration! Though mild, our celebration of this fools' day is a relic and reminder of the important values of humor, humility and foolishness. Popes and church councils for the past several hundreds of years have not had to condemn the activities of this feast of fools. Such a fact is well worth our attention. Over the centuries this feast was condemned for drunkenness and other unbecoming behavior of people, laity and clergy alike. For example, on this feast of fools, social roles were exchanged for a day. The lay brother in the monastery became the abbot and ruled from his throne for the day. Some layman was chosen to be pope-for-a-day and received the applause of the crowds. Charades by the people made fun of the king, queen, bishop, mayor, mother superior or anyone in the position of authority and power.

Strong as were the statements of the bishops and councils, the feast continued. What church councils found impossible to stop, the industrial revolution achieved; what papal pronouncements failed to alter, the Reformation eliminated: the feast of foolishness. While today we have a variety of holidays, we are, perhaps, less human and holy because we lack a holiday for silliness. Act like a fool at work on April 1 and see what happens to you! Imitate the personality of your boss with some humorous horseplay on April Fools' Day, and on April 2 you will likely be looking for a new job! On the assembly line, in the corporate office and in religion, little room is left for humor or foolishness. Sadly, we might add, there is little room for these two virtues in our hearts as well!

When the foolishness of this feast was suppressed, all that remained were practical jokes. These, along with the holiday itself, were given over to children. Today, children are the custodians of this ancient and religious celebration while adults are busy with matters of consequence. What we lost was more than some ancient feast; we further lost a valuable tool for wholesomeness: humor. We also misplaced one of the signs of the kingdom of the Spirit. This sign was the humble ability to laugh at ourselves and at power. Our age values production, prestige and power. As a result, we do not choose silly saints as patrons upon which to pattern our lives. In Old English, the word "silly" originally meant happy, humble, innocent and of low station. The word also meant low intelligence or senselessness. Early Christians were silly saints not because they were senseless but because they had the good sense to seek innocence, simplicity and humility.

Jesus, with insightful knowledge of the ageless hunger of the human heart for power and pomp, insisted that His disciples must wash one another's feet. Those who wished to be at the top must also be at the bottom, serving the needs of their brothers and sisters. He knew of our almost incurable addiction to honor and power and so offered a cure: humble service and foolishness. If we find it difficult today to joke and have fun with those who have power over us, could it be that they do not consider themselves to be our brothers or sisters? Could it also be that we do not view ourselves as their brothers and sisters? Humor and fun are able to dance in harmony with respect and honor, but they can never dance as partners with pomp and power! Where there is love, there is God and, we might add, humor as well. The washing of the feet of the apostles at the Last Supper was more than symbolic. This act of humble service is filled with meaning for anyone who has set foot to the Way. Jesus insisted that His friends must submit their soles into His hands. That last evening together had been heavy with the sacred and solemn, but it was to conclude with a smile! If you have ever had your feet washed or rubbed, then you know how ticklish is this action. Jesus, on His knees, must have looked up and smiled as He saw His friends attempting to suppress the normal expression of being tickled: "As I have served you in humility, so you must each serve one another in such a low station. I know that it is silly, but such is the kingdom of fools and clowns. Tomorrow, I will be no more than a joke to the crowds and the soldiers. Your day, my friends, will also come. Learn well this lesson that I teach you this evening."

Saint Paul called Christians "Fools for Christ," silly people who by their lives would invite the martyrdom of laughter and ridicule. They would be a people whose values, lifestyles and beliefs would merit only a smile from the wise and sophisticated of the world. His disciples would feel honored to suffer some bloody martyr's death, yet we often find it so difficult to bear ridicule and laughter for our beliefs.

Perhaps if we did not have to be so "respectable," we might be more free and so able to enjoy life to a greater degree. If we were not so "proper," we might discover God in unlikely places. Some time ago, I read the reflections on life by an 85-year-old woman from Louisville, Kentucky. Nadine Stair took a look at her life and made these insightful observations:

If I had my life to live over, I'd dare to make more mistakes next time. I'd relax, I would limber up. I would be sillier than I had been this trip. I would take fewer things seriously. I would take more chances. I would climb more mountains and swim more rivers. I would eat more ice cream and less beans. I would perhaps have more actual troubles, but I'd have fewer imaginary ones. You see, I'm one of those people who live sensibly and sanely hour after hour, day after day. Oh, I've had my moments and if I had it to do over again, I'd have more of them. In fact, I'd try to have nothing else. Just moments, one after another, instead of living so many years ahead of each day. I've been one of those persons who never goes anywhere without a thermometer, a hot water bottle, a raincoat and a parachute. If I had to do it again, I would travel lighter than I have. If I had my life to live again, I would start barefoot earlier in the spring and stay that way later in the fall. I would go to more dances. I would ride more merry-go-rounds. I would pick more daisies.

If it is necessary for us to bear the heavy burden of always being "proper," then we will find it very difficult to go barefoot and to live like children, for whom it says the gates of heaven open wide. We perhaps need less "respect" and more humility. We need fewer committees and more clowns. A good clown or fool is able to show us how to laugh at ourselves. Such an ability is humble prayer that drives out demons like pride, vanity, stuffiness, rigidity and pomp. When we are able to find mirth in the middle of our muddled lives, we will also find the mystical. Humor and foolishness make it possible to forget the self. Silliness is but to be free of the self and to be free is to taste salvation.

Salvation, or enlightenment, comes when we are free of the self, the ego. It is to be absent to the self, or as the Zen spiritual masters might say, "No one is at home!" From the thousand-and-one tales of the Desert Fathers (early Christians who went to the desert to live a religious lifestyle) comes a delightful story about this basic principle of the inner-life. Once a famous spiritual master, together with his small group of disciples, was traveling in the desert. The only place to stay one night was in an abandoned pagan temple. As the disciples prepared to go to sleep, the old master knelt in front of the statue of the temple god. First, he prayed with tears and groans, then with long hymns of praise. Next, he jumped to his feet and pelted the statue with rocks and insults, only to fall to his knees again in long, beautiful prayers of praise. Over and over, he repeated these contradictory actions. Finally, one of his young disciples said to him, "Abba, father, why are you acting in such a strange way?" The old man replied, "What way?" The disciple answered, "Well, you insult and throw rocks at the god, and then you praise it only to return to throwing more rocks." "And young man," said the master, "what did the god do about my actions?" The disciple answered, "Nothing at all, master." "Exactly," said the old master, "this god did nothing because he is not home, he is not present in this statue. So it should be with you. Praise, regardless of how beautiful, or insults, be they hard as rocks, should not change your actions if you are not at home to your self! This is far from easy, my son, but with practice you may learn to be absent from yourself so that you can be present to the Self, the Divine Self within."

As we feel more and more comfortable with play and with the prayer of humble fun, of foolishness, we might learn to die to self through humor, so as to make more room for the Divine Self within us, to be absent to insults (to the shower of sticks and stones), and to praise (in the parade of roses). If we could find time to be a little foolish, we might find life to be happier and more filled with the Divine Presence. We

might also find God in the silly and funny things of
life. As Dr. Seuss says, "From there to here, from
here to there, funny things are everywhere!"

A Fool's Prayer

Father and God of Fools,
    Lord of Clowns and Smiling Saints,
    I rejoice in this playful prayer
    that You are a God of laughter and of tears.
Blessed are You, for You have rooted within me
    the gifts of humor, lightheartedness and mirth.
With jokes and comedy, You cause my heart to sing
    as laughter is made to flow out of me.

I am grateful that Your Son, Jesus,
    who was this world's master of wit,
    daily invites me to be a fool for Your sake,
    to embrace the madness
    of Your prophets, holy people and saints.
I delight in that holy madness
    which becomes the very medicine
    to heal the chaos of the cosmos
    since it calls each of us
    out of the hum-drumness of daily life
    into joy, adventure,
    and, most of all, into freedom.

I, who am so easily tempted to barter my freedom
for tiny speckles of honor and power,
am filled with gratitude that Your Son's very life
has reminded me to value only love,
the communion with other persons and with You,
and to balance honor with humor.

With circus bands and organ grinders,
with fools, clowns, court-jesters and comics,
with high-spirited angels and saints,
I too join the fun and foolishness of life,
so that Your holy laughter
may ring out to the edges of the universe.

Blessed are You, Lord my God,
who invites me to be a holy fool.

Amen+

Magic Magi
Gifting Prayer

Praying is frequently called an art. As with all art, it is the result of a talent that is a birth-gift. All prayerful communion with God is gift; it is not something that we achieve so much as something that we prepare ourselves to receive and accept. This chapter deals not with praying as a gift but with gifting as prayer. In the last chapter we reflected on becoming a child again and becoming lost in playfulness and foolishness. The feast of children, in Europe and Asia, is Epiphany, and their patrons are the three wise men. As we reflect upon the art of gifting as prayer, we can find no better place to begin than with those three mysterious magi who gifted the infant Jesus.

The magi were priestly wise men whose number over the ages has varied from three to twelve. Today we think of them as three in number. They came, we are told, from the East following a star that proclaimed the birth of a new King, a Wonder-Worker and Prince of Peace. We can wonder what the Gospel story would have been like if these magi had come not from the East but the West.

If they had come from the West, these men would not have been kings but rather professors, and no doubt they would have been department heads from different universities. Then again, knowing our Western mentality, we would have probably sent a committee, an adoration committee. This adoration committee would have been composed of our most intelligent people. Such a committee would have proposed practical gifts for this poor family that was living in such dire poverty. These modern magi of the West would have come bearing gifts of boxes of groceries, warm clothing and perhaps even a propane stove. As Western wise ones, they would have thought of something more useful than incense for poor people who were living in a barn! Instead of myrrh or perfume, they would have presented to Jesus, Mary and Joseph insulated underwear. To our Western way of logic, to give to the poor golden gifts instead of the practical necessities of life smacks of stupidity. But then again, the first magi were from the East and not from the West. Also, they were wise men and therefore men of wisdom.

The East as a civilization, because it is much older than the West, perhaps understands better the briefness of this mortal life. The people of the East know that it is necessary to acquire as much pleasure from life as possible. Time is far too short to delay the enjoyment of it. Indeed, there will be practical matters to attend to in life. We must have homes in which to live, food to eat and clothing for our bodies. But we have souls as well. This spiritual or inner person also has needs to be nourished. Just as the body has needs, so has the heart. We have a need for the incenses and perfumes of life and the gold of beauty. True wisdom is found in the proper care of the entire person, of the outer and inner person.

Moses was one of the magi of history. Jesus quoted the mage (singular of magi) Moses when He said, "Man does not live on bread alone" (Lk 4:4). The three magi — Casper, Melchior and Balthasar — understood the wisdom of Moses, for it was also the wisdom of China, India, and the entire Orient. What differences would appear in our lives if we could also make such wisdom part of our personal philosophy of life. We do need bread, but we also have needs for music and poetry. We need bridges and butter, but we also need beauty. Simply to have all the necessities of life and three meals a day will not bring us happiness. Happiness is hidden in the unnecessary and in those impractical things that bring delight to the inner person.

The magi knew the truth that it is folly to work so hard becoming successful in life that you have no time left with which to enjoy life. So an attitude of being constantly busy in efforts to make more and more money or in the effort to bring about the Kingdom is folly to the wisdom of the East and also to the wisdom of God. When we lack proper time for the simple pleasures of life, for the enjoyment of eating, drinking, playing, creating, visiting friends and watching children at play, then we have missed the purpose of life. Not on bread alone do we live but on all these human and heart-hungry luxuries.

One way that the East expresses the importance of simple pleasures as luxuries for the enjoyment of life is in the tea ceremony. The simple pleasure of drinking tea together in a small rustic teahouse in a garden is indeed very Eastern and very foreign to our Western minds. The drinking of tea is not merely for refreshment but is also a form of sociability. It is a unifying element whenever friends meet. The tea is sipped in appreciation, little by little, and not consumed cup by cup. Time is taken to taste the flavor, to enjoy the scent and to take delight in the cups themselves. Tea drinking is a symbol of how life itself is to be enjoyed, a sip at a time. Whether you are watching the sunset or observing a painting, it must be seen at leisure and never with a hasty glance. We should drink in life, sip by sip, with thoughtfulness and an open heart until slowly the inner significance sinks into our hearts. The example of this one Eastern custom should remind us that our problem is twofold: the modern American emphasis on practicality and the necessity to rush through everything. But we need both the beautiful in our lives and the time to sip it slowly.

The question upon the tip of your heart is, "Well and good, but who has time for sipping, especially in these days?" Also, we tend to look upon persons who are not production-oriented as being lazy. That the people of the East have found poetry and the non-productive as essential experiences of life is not a sign that they are lazy. Indeed, we of the West look upon those who prefer the enjoyment of life to the achievement of "great" things as lacking in motivation. As children we learned in Aesop's fable what happened to the pleasure-seeking grasshopper who spent his summer in the enjoyment of life instead of working hard in preparation for winter. The Easterner, however, is far from being lazy and will put enormous energy into living, eating and the enjoyment of life. Look through a Chinese cookbook and you will see the time and effort that is necessary to truly prepare an oriental dish. The senses are not fed with delight without time and effort. The real paradox is that the East and not the West is materialistic. But the materialism of the East is just that — a full enjoyment of the material, earthy aspects of the world. The materialism of the West is not an enjoyment of material things but the collection of material objects. Implied in our stockpiling of "things" is the future enjoyment of them, but the future never seems to come.

We need to learn how to enjoy material things and by our enjoyment of them to become "en-tangled," engaged with them. We need to get into the center of life instead of living only on the edges of it, on the surface of what we see, taste, touch and hear. This entanglement or engagement with material things is truly a love affair with the Divine Mystery who is forever One with matter. As Teilhard de Chardin said, "By Your Incarnation, O Lord, all matter has become incarnate!" A holistic spirituality implies such an engagement with material things so that sensible pleasure comes from our love affair with Him. The primary need of the human spirit is to take pleasure in God present in all creation.

Our religious historical formation has made us suspicious of enjoying the natural, not to mention that the moral theology of the three little pigs warns us against taking pleasure in the luxuries of life. According to this formation, eating, sleeping, making love and the other uses of the senses are not so much to be enjoyed as to be endured. We fear the sensual enjoyment of the natural lest it steal us away from the supernatural. A story is told about an old Jesuit priest who was on retreat. He was reading a book of poetry when another priest walked by and saw what type of book he was reading. The other priest paused and said, "Father, that book will not save your soul." The other priest looked up, smiled and replied, "Yes, I know, but it will make my soul worth saving." We too need special things like poetry and music, sunsets and tea cups to make our souls worth saving.

Can we learn some daily wisdom from our three magi and perhaps give useless and impractical gifts? Can we give gifts that will enrich the hearts of those who receive them? Erma Bombeck says, "As a mother, I would love to get a gift for once that didn't have a warranty card with it!" Not only at Christmas time but at the numerous other opportunities for gift-giving, can we select our gifts as did the three kings? And in our living of life, can we also find time for the luxury of sipping the beautiful things that surround us?

Along with the magi's gifts of gold, incense, and perfume, there were other gifts. As travelers from the East, those three wise men manifested another oriental custom and an aspect of the spiritual enjoyment of life, which was their concern for courtesy. In the East, even the Middle East, ceremonial behavior that showed a consideration for the feelings of others is considered a high priority. The magi's visit to King Herod was not only to ask directions. Such a visit would have been in keeping with their tradition of showing proper respect to the local ruler while passing through the territory. When they arrived at the destination of their long journey, the adoration before Jesus was part of the same cultural attitude. Adoration, bowing and other such manifestations of gracious behavior seem out of place for modern democratic people. Adoration, which is physical in expression, has fallen upon evil days of late. Since worship is a mirror of our daily lives, we should not be surprised. Gracious behavior among ourselves has also fallen upon evil days. Since we fail to show reverence to one another in the daily flow of life, we should not be that surprised that a spirit of deep reverence is absent from our prayer and worship. The ceremonial behavior of Melchior and his two fellow magi holds another gift for us, and we would do well to reflect upon it.

For countless centuries, it seems, the East has been crowded with people living very close to one another. Cities had narrow streets where merchants and travelers were elbow to elbow. This closeness has created the need for a sacrament of consideration and courtesy. Whenever people are crowded closely together in customer-filled stores at Christmas time or in modern apartment houses, they need to remember that we live on more than just bread. Our lives are also fed by kind words and gracious behavior. We are nourished by expressions like "excuse me" and other such simple courtesies. Our spirits are also richly fed on compliments and praise; nourished by consideration as well as whole wheat bread. Rudeness, the absence of the sacrament of consideration, is but another mark that our time-is-money society is lacking in spirituality if not also in its enjoyment of life. Gracious behavior is due to the elderly, to the stranger and to those who serve us. I do not here refer to house servants but to persons in service-related occupations. In countless ways we are waited upon, served and cared for in our modern society. These service-persons are just that — persons and not machines. We express our belief in their personhood by the sacrament of courtesy. As well, we are enlivened and healed by that expression of respect, dignity and gracious kindness that flows from the heart.

Finally, we reflect that the magi were not simply wise men, but by their very name they were also magicians! They did not pull rabbits out of their hats to entertain the child Jesus nor did they amaze the holy family with card tricks, but they did work magic! Their gifts of perfume, incense and gold transformed the humble surroundings of that poor family into glittering glory. Surprise, joy and beauty were their gifts to the child and His parents. Their gracious behavior turned refugees into royalty regardless of the poor surroundings. We who so often live lives of drab duty and of practical necessity need that kind of magic in our lives. We need impractical gifts if our spirits are to be fed. If our precious money is spent

79

for those things that delight the soul, that feed the heart and cause the spirit to smile, is that money really wasted? We who often feel like machines need to be reminded by courtesy and gentle manners that we are royal people, that we are people and not "things." Indeed, we need the magic of the magi. We do not have to take a twelve-week correspondence course in "How to be a Magician" to perform some of the same magic that the magi did. What we do need is more madness than magic. We need that crazy sense of values that says, "Man does not live on bread alone but on beautiful things, perfume, red wines, roses in winter, good books, incense, respect, kindness and the time to enjoy them all slowly, sip by sip." Such magic is mystical and can truly transform our lives into the beautiful and the holy. Such magic is at the heart of the mystery of Christ and the core of the Kingdom, for was not Jesus the Archmage of them all?

A Prayer for That Which
Bread Alone Cannot Satisfy

Lord of Great Richness,
  we are indeed a practical people
  who always put "first" things first.
And yet, it seems, we may not know
  that which is truly first.
You have showed us
  how we are not to live on bread alone,
  and yet we find it so difficult
  to believe in the value
  of the "useless" but beautiful things of life:
  of flowers, gifts, art and music,
  of play, poetry and celebration.
We need to learn — and You are the prime teacher —
  that the practical things of life
  are enhanced by the impractical,
  and that without these beautiful things
  our souls and spirits become barren.

Help me to "waste" money
  on that which is beautiful,
  to "waste" time on those enriching things
  which have little monetary value
  and to rejoice in their many charms.
May I see in the textbook of creation
  that You fill the earth
  with beauty as well as with practicality;
  that even in the useful
  lies the purely ornamental
  and that in seeing Your holy and artistic design,
  I may, with Your grace,
  do and be the same.

Amen+

Suffering —
The School of Prayer

Good wine and saints have more in common than meets the eye. As a college student, I discovered the English poet and writer Hilaire Belloc. One of his creative works I enjoyed was this short verse:

> Wherever the Christian sun doth shine
> there's always laughter and good red wine,
> at least I always found it so,
> Benedicamus Domino. (Let us bless the Lord)

Belloc's poem could be paraphrased to read:

> Wherever the Christian sun doth shine
> there's always laughter and many tears
> at least I always found it so,
> Benedicamus Domino.

This paraphrase breaks the poetic rhyme, but it does speak to the reality of life with its share of suffering and pain, tears and laughter. Pain and suffering, whether physical or mental, are the "stuff" of our existence. While part of daily life, suffering and pain usually are not freely chosen. At best, we attempt to learn how to embrace them with a minimum of complaint. Often the circumstances of our daily lives force us to reflect upon the presence of pain and suffering and their co-existence with a compassionate God. We often conclude this reflection by making some "religious" statement, like "Well, it's all part of God's will! Someday I will understand, but for now it is a mystery." Face to face with such a cosmic mystery, we respond with a large dose of faith and smile as we grit our teeth and bear the pain. Suffering and pain are never easy to explain, for they raise too many unanswered questions.

On the evening of the first Easter, two disciples of the rabbi from Nazareth were walking along the road towards the village of Emmaus. As they walked along, they were joined by a stranger. They presented to the stranger the question of suffering as they struggled with the crucifixion and death of their spiritual master. Their quesion was timeless, as current today as it was on that dusty road to Emmaus: "Why?" To this question, the stranger, who was the risen Christ, responded with an unusual question that hid within it an answer: "Did not the Messiah have to undergo all this so as to enter into His glory?" The response was not a reason to excuse the suffering, but rather to say how else could He, the Messiah, achieve His glory? Without the suffering of His Passion, the gentle rabbi from Nazareth would have remained simply Jesus and would never have become *the Christ*, the Cosmic Lord of Glory. The brutal death and the resurrection transfigured the wonder-worker from Galilee permanently into divine glory. Also, it would only be after His painful sufferings that the words and works of Jesus would begin to bear fruit.

Bearing fruit is a clue to understanding the problem of pain. Human life, like all of creation, is a series of reflections — mirrors inside of mirrors — all connected in a spiral of interlocking systems. What is true for Nature is true for human nature. Fruitfulness in persons has its pattern in the fruitfulness of nature, which brings us back to the opening statement about what saints and good wine have in common. In the growing of grapes we find a beautiful parallel with the process of growth in you and me.

The pruning of the grapevine is a mirror-reflection of the activity of pain and suffering in our lives. The cutting and removing of sections of the grapevine during its dormant period is one of the most important aspects of raising the good grapes which are necessary to produce good wine. The wise vineyard keeper knows how to prune, to cut away, and when to do it. He understands that the purpose of this "destructive" act is to make the vines grow fewer, but better, grapes. Those vines that have felt the knife in pruning will produce grapes of greater maturity and of greater potential than the vines which have not suffered. When grapevines are too successful and produce too many grapes (a term called "over-cropping" in the grape industry), they will soon only produce thin, watery wine! Here, I am reminded of a line from a poem by G.K. Chesterton, who was a friend of Hilaire Belloc. The poem was about Noah and the great flood, and it went something like this: "I don't care where the water goes as long as it doesn't get in the wine!" Watery wine is as unappealing as watered-down people.

A grapevine that has been properly pruned will also produce grapes in which the acid and sugar content is perfectly balanced. As a result, the wine that comes from such grapes will be full-bodied, beautiful in color, and rich in aroma. Sometimes the usual pruning is not enough. On occasion, even after the vine has been pruned, it will continue to over-produce. When this happens, the vineyard keeper must thin out the vine, sometimes removing whole grape clusters. A part of the crop is sacrificed so that the remaining grapes will be of superior quality. And there are even times when, for the sake of a good harvest, the entire vine is radically cut back — all of it, and all the way to the ground!

> NOTE: In case you are wondering at this point if you are reading the wrong book, allow me to reassure you. This is indeed not the National Grape Growers' Manual. So please continue to read on . . . .

A skilled foreman in a vineyard knows how to prune each type of vine because each type of grape requires its own special care. He is unable to be a democrat, treating all the same when it comes to pruning. Each vine will need personal attention. To ensure the best quality from the grapes, the foreman may vary the number of spurs on each vine. ("Spurs" is the term for the wood left after the pruning.) For example, if he is pruning the Chenin Blanc vine, he will not allow more than twelve spurs. If he is tending the French Colombard grape, he will allow fourteen. In general, the rule is that vines with larger grapes are pruned more! Excellent, full-bodied and perfectly balanced wine can only come from vines that have felt the sharp knife of the pruner.

Suffering in our lives, if it is as creative as the pruning of the vine, will produce greater potential within us. Pruning is the rule for grapes as well as for saints, for heroes and heroines. While it seems to make good sense to prune grapevines, we are not that convinced of the benefit when it is our turn to be pruned. Jesus, before His own death, spoke to His disciples about how God was the foreman in the vineyard and knew how to trim down the good vines so that they would produce more life: "I am the real vine, and My Father is the gardener. Every barren branch of mine He cuts away; and every fruitful branch He prunes to make it more fruitful still . . ." (John 15:1). Jesus called Himself "the vine," and it

86

seems that it was necessary that in death He be radically cut back — all the way to the ground — so that a superior and glorious harvest might be produced in Him.

What was true for Him is equally true for you and me. When does trouble come knocking at our door? Usually just when everything seems to be going well; when we are really producing (or do they call that over-cropping?). Sickness, pain and trouble come in ten thousand shapes and sizes, and they can be dead-ending and produce nothing in our lives but more pain.

The cutting away of part of the grapevine is creative, but all pain and suffering is not creative. We can find it difficult to separate good suffering from bad suffering if we live in a society which is in hectic pursuit of happiness. In such a society suffering is the enemy of happiness. Viewed as an enemy, it will be resisted and fled from at every opportunity. An unhealthy religion will tend to romanticize suffering and make sterile, non-creative suffering into a desirable goal. Pierre Boulez defines what life is about when he says, "The goal of life is not happiness, it is living!" Living cannot exist without suffering; ask any healthy, fully-alive grapevine! Religious symbols such as the cross certainly are not intended to lead us to worship pain or suffering. Rather such images should remind us that if we seek to experience life to the fullest, then we must be willing to embrace suffering. We cannot escape suffering in this life. And so, instead of attempting to flee from it, we should enter into it with creativity.

Early in his singing career, Bing Crosby was struggling to find his own distinctive style of singing. At that time he was an unknown entertainer and was part of a singing group. In the early thirties he became sick when nodules, small lumps, formed on his vocal cords. When he recovered, the nodules remained. The result was a most unique voice which Bing described as the voice of some teenager singing in a rain barrel. Because of his sickness he found that he now had a distinctive singing style and that style soon made him a star. His suffering was not destructive but creative and bore great fruit. Suffering is like manure; it can be unseemly and offensive, or it can be the "stuff" out of which great productivity comes.

There is a story about a man who was suffering from extreme emotional anxiety. His anxiety was the result of a recurring dream. Night after night, he dreamed the same dream, awakening each morning with a terrible headache and completely exhausted. Seeking help, he went to a psychiatrist. The doctor asked what it was that he dreamed and the man answered, "Each night, I dream that I am trying to open a large door. I feel that it is important that I go through the doorway. The door is a large, glass one and there is a single word printed on it. All night I pull and pull at the door but it will not open. At the end of the dream I am exhausted and collapse at the bottom of the door." After several minutes of deep thought the psychiatrist asked, "What is the word that is printed on the glass door?" The man answered: "Push."

Most of us spend our time pulling against reality; the reality of pain and suffering as an integral part of life. But if we would "push," flow inward with the mystery of suffering, we might find that it would open all sorts of doors for us. When we are able to flow with suffering, we move with it and through it. When we reject suffering or war against it, we end up a victim of anxiety and exhaustion as did the man in the simple story. Suffering and pain are creative when they lead to the growth of the human spirit and the ability to experience life. Such suffering calls forth from us, as it does from the Chenin Blanc vines, a new and greater potential for life. If the physical or emotional pain that enters our lives is to be creative and fruitful, we should preface it with inner pain and personal prayer. Before Jesus shed blood, He sweat blood. We might wonder which of the two experiences of Jesus was more difficult. Which suffering was the greater and deeper pain for Jesus to bear: the night prayer in the olive garden of Gethsemane or the crucifixion? Perhaps the suffering of one's spirit, one's very soul, in surrender to God in the pain of a Gethsemane night is more profound.

Is there room in your prayer life for a Gethsemane Prayer? We might find it valuable if the Church had a special feast day to celebrate just the mystery 'of Gethsemane. That feast day celebration might help us to remember to include such a prayer in our lives. What is Gethsemane Prayer? It is not the prayer of community or even of confirmation, but rather one of loneliness and doubt. It is a prayer of preparation for the future because in it we embrace and accept the suffering that will come. In some ways it is the prayer where we ask God to send us a cross!

About ten years ago I made a prayer pilgrimage that took me through Europe, Israel and India. I spent several months in Israel, a great part of that time living and praying in the Old City of Jerusalem. Each morning and night I would go out onto the roof of the hostel where I was staying and pray. The view was magnificent since the pilgrim hostel was located near the site of the old Temple area. One day, as the sun was setting, I was finishing my evening prayers. The light of the setting sun illuminated in glowing gold the Mount of Olives when I suddenly prayed aloud: "Father, send to me a cross as You did to Your Son, Jesus." The petition came suddenly and spontaneously to my lips. As soon as I heard what I had said, I was gripped with fear. I wanted to reach up and take back those words that hung still and clear in the twilight of that ancient city. I wished that there were some way to erase their existence, but there was none. My fear was replaced by feelings of shame. I was ashamed that I was too much of a coward to desire to follow completely in the footsteps of my Lord. Fear and shame were joined by another emotion, conviction. I was convinced that God had heard my spontaneous prayer and that *this* prayer would be answered! As the lingering light of the setting sun began to disappear and the purple and blue shades of night flowed over the Old City, I prayed that when and however my prayer was answered that I would have the courage and ability to make that cross a personal instrument of growth and new life. I was already apprehensive of my pilgrimage to India, fearful that I might not return to the States alive. In more ways than one, the darkness grew around me as I stood on that rooftop. I wanted to flow with the approaching suffering, and as I let go of trying to prevent it or cancel it, a sense of peaceful harmony filled my heart. Two months later, on Christmas morning, outside the Indian city of Varanasi, I fell deathly sick with hepatitis. My prayer had been answered, but the Gethsemane Prayer on the rooftop had prepared me. Forced by the sickness into inactivity, I had to sit still, be quiet and rest. I had unlimited time to reflect. As a result, the sickness was one of the most prayerful and fruitful times of my entire pilgrimage.

Each of our lives should have room for that midnight garden prayer if we are to make suffering creative, growthful and productive. To pray alone that kind of embracing prayer will prepare us for what must come to us when everything is going so well — perhaps too well — since such over-cropping success leads to empty, watered-down lives. Each of us, at one time or another, will need to be pruned if we wish our lives to be of superior quality. But doesn't pruning hurt? If the vines of the French Colombard grape could be given lips, they might cry out in pain as the foreman cuts away on them: "Why us? We are hard-working, good vines that produce only great clusters of grapes. Why are we selected to suffer?" But then again, perhaps the vines understand how the universe really works. Instead of protesting, they may — like Christ in Gethsemane — embrace their pain because they understand the inner laws of the universe that call for sacrifice and for suffering. They understand, being so much closer to the earth than we, that they will soon bear superior clusters of grapes . . . better than before. It is we who are slow to comprehend what life and sacrifice are all about.

The suffering of Christ was more than creative; it was also sacrificial. Our daily sufferings and pains hold the seed of sacrifice for us. Sacrifice is an essential part of the life pattern. Sacrifice is also part of "praying always," which is the lifestyle of any follower of Christ. The simple surrender to the reality of some pain does not make that suffering a sacrifice. Sacrifice is gifting God in return for the gifts we have received. Those who practice sacrifice as part of their spirituality understand the inner nature of relationships. When we are gifted, as we are each day with countless gifts from a generous God, we are united in gratitude to the Divine Mystery for such expressions of love. Whenever we are gifted by life or love, a certain "link" is forged between the giver and the receiver. Psychologically, a stronger bond is formed by giving than by receiving. If we are eager to deepen our love relationship with God, then we should seek ways to "gift" our Lord with precious gifts. When we take our suffering and own it and do not attempt to

91

escape from it, that suffering becomes a precious part of us. Since it involves the inner pain of the soul, such suffering is truly a deep part of us. The Prayer of Gethsemane is the presentation to God of the gift of ourselves — past, present and future. When we are able to lift up to God as gift the pruned part of ourselves, we find that the mystic union between God and ourselves has deepened. The purpose of every sacrifice is to forge a bond or link with the Divine Mystery. The prayer of sacrifice is an interchange of giving and receiving, which is the flow of all true love. We often feel that the origin of sacrifice was the fear of the gods or God. For some that may have been true, but for others, sacrifice was a mystical experience. The sacrifice of personal suffering offered the possibility of an authentic "Holy" Communion, a communion of receiving and giving. The most eloquent "thank you" is the gift of ourselves. The sufferings of Christ are for us a pattern, not only for a life of struggle and pain, but also for a life of gratitude, of Eucharist.

When the honeymoon is over — when sickness and difficulties come to our family, when we lose jobs, fail to acquire that which we greatly desire, suffer the loss of someone we dearly love — when these and other sufferings come to us, we should remember our cousins in creation, the grapevines. We must learn to trust that we will be pruned at the "proper" time by the Divine Vineyard Keeper and that the primary purpose of this suffering is creative. Each pain in life is but a preparation for the final and ultimate pruning when we will be radically cut back — all the way to the ground in our own death. We can embrace that last great adventure without fear if we have, without fear, allowed the divine pruning knife to touch our lives and our loves. From this last and most creative pruning of all, we will come forth in the full-bodied perfection of our resurrection.

92

A Prayer for Insight into Suffering

Lord, my God, Incomprehensible One,
  Your sacrament of suffering,
  the mystery of pain,
  is an integral part of my life.
I have at times been offered the cup of bitterness
  so that I may share in the sorrow
  that was freely embraced by Your Son, Jesus,
  and so that I may help to heal
  the sickness that plagues our planet.

I thank You for opportunities to explore,
  with those around me and with all the world,
  the profound puzzle of pain.
May I seek only the fullness of life
  and not reject the element of pain
  inherent in all growth
  and essential in each search for wholeness.

As a disciple of Christ,
  I follow in the footsteps
  of a suffering savior,
  asking that this pain
  have special meaning for me
  and for all the earth.

Blessed are You, Lord my God,
  who shares pain and suffering
  as part of the mystery of life.

Amen+

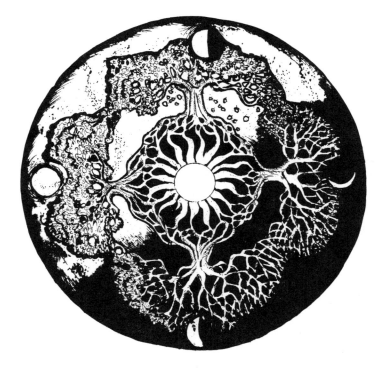

Hurrying —
A Hindrance to the Holy

Greetings, Fellow Criminals!
The salutation's a lucky guess.
Half the population breaks the law;
the limit on speed is 55.
Law breakers — a salutation that's an easy bet
addressing Kansans and Missourians —
of them, 70% break that law of limit.

Kansas with its long, lethargic miles of flat farm land:
why linger? Hurry-up to get from here to there —
and from there to here.
Now, California, Indiana and Idaho, much more to
see—
and yet, there, as here,
we're in a hurry to get from here to there —
and there to here.
Not 70 but 99 & 44/100% pulled over to the curb,
if speed limits were placed on eating lunch,
drinking coffee, drying dishes, making love and
praying.

Our lifestyle is R & R: rushing and running.
We've been programmed in Pampers to hurry.

"Hurry-up and eat your breakfast . . . you'll be late."
"Hurry-up and get dressed . . . everyone is waiting."
"Hurry-up, students . . . only five minutes left."
And now, today, when the little round light
turns from red to green — before the electric eclipse is
over —
honk-honk, hurry-up, hurry-up.

Brother Marx was wrong; it's not religion —
haste is the opium of the masses.
Haste makes waste, wrong again, haste makes fun.
Shoot up with speed, another fix of stimulation —
Hurry, hurry,
double your pleasure, double your fun
double your speed and get it done!

We pause, catch our breath, panting a pious petition—
"Lord, teach us how to pray . . . in a hurry!"

Water in acid, haste in prayer, don't mix!
Hurry hurts our hearts and haste poisons our prayer.
Haste, in Old English-Saxon tongue meant violence,
once upon a time.
The meaning's changed, the effect's the same.
Haste is violence . . . to our prayer —
haste is violence . . . to our health,
to our marriages, friendships, and Contemplative
communion.
We deplore violence on the screen and in the streets.
Then why promote haste at home
and rushing on the road?

Our neighbor, Wyoming, is out to change the double-
nickel law,
too slow a speed for empty space.
Nothing's between Rock Springs and Cheyenne —
so why dally over sagebrush and barren land?

Truckers, coffee cups raised on high, holler, "Up with Wyoming!"
"Hurrah!" shout tourists, cramped in their campers
while neighboring states all applaud.
Who . . . who has time to slow down?
The Kingdom is at hand — work, while the light lasts!
Who has time to slow down?
It is the will of the people —
"More fast food and service instamatic!
Ban radar, rather than the Bomb."

Whirlin' round in the revolving door of Life's Department Store,
we hear the Voice of God whispering in the whirl,
"I will lead her into the desert and speak to her heart.
She shall respond there as in the days of her youth."
Into the desert to find a different pace —
in the desert . . . too hot to hurry, silly . . . in the sun to run.
Take your time, move s-l-o-w-l-y.
Watch the camel, learn a lesson, measure well the journey.
"Lord, can't we pray at home? Why lead us into the desert?"
"Why, my children?
Hustle, hustle, is the music of the marketplace, that's why —
Hurry, hurry, is the song of the city, that's why."

In the desert, ageless, clockless, still as sagebrush —
all moves at lizard's speed.
Time to sit and once again to hear.
"God speaks slowly," say the Ancient Ones —
a word an hour, a sentence a century.
Those in a hurry . . . hear not!
Jesus in the desert, said Mark, "absorbed in prayer"
Jesus in the desert, led by the Spirit —

soaked up in silence and sand,
responded as in His Youth.
In the desert, no hurry to hear, no rush to respond.
Friends . . . contemplative prayer, in the Sinai or in
Cincinnati —
always has the slow scent of sagebrush.

Why is it hard to pray?
Well, there's no time to pray.
It's hurry, hurry, you'll be late.
Hurry is a habit and we have grown to hate to wait.
"Let's get this show on the road . . . let's go, what's
the delay?"
Speed is our Holy Spirit, a Virtue, not a vice.
Twice as much to do, so learn to double up.
"Blessed is the man who can do two things at once,"
open his mail and answer the phone,
brush his teeth and balance his budget,
watch TV and read the paper . . .
Why is this a virtue, and not a vice?

Words, like eggs, hold secrets, hide truths.
Drugstore, daily words, like haste,
once upon a time meaning violence . . .
Why is hurry a virtue and not a vice?
Take a word, a yellow word . . . SLOW . . .
Turn back the clock centuries.
Slow first meant not less speed, but stupid!
If you're slow in getting the point, slow with the answer —
you're stupid, dull and witless.
Smart people, we all know,
are fast with the answer, first to finish, swift with
solutions.
Smart people can do two, three things at once.
Ah, so easy and so swift, and fast . . . .
So, who wants to be slow and dull
and stand at the rear of the class?

Hurry-up and prove your worth!
Busy days and speedy answers,
all status signs of Brilliant people.

Do you want to pray? Slow Down!
Eat your green peas one by one —
Chew your food, don't wash it down.
Sip your wine and words slowly,
linger long on a friendship, pause and ponder, take
your time.
Have the courage to cancel — the stomach to say
"no"
so as to have the time
to taste your life, your loves and the 57 flavors of
prayer.

Taste . . . Life . . . Slowly.
And beware, the Devil of the Power Drive
is purring near your ear —
resist the temptation to rush around —
giving Life but a harried glance,
taking only samples of friendship,
only samples of prayer and daily life.
Take your time, Friends —
for in the ordinary hides the Extra-ordinary,
in the daily, you'll find the Divine . . .
"Blessed are those who live slowly for they shall see God."

Stop, look and listen . . .
We always overlook when we overbook.
Braniff, Continental, and You and I overbook our
days.
Too many events, too many things to do —
hurry, hurry, and finish, then we'll pray.
Hurry, hurry, then, job done, we taste good times.
But when we "overbook" our days, who's left
behind?

Who's left at the gate when all things significant have
been seated?
The Divine Beloved, our Secret Friend —
who never pushes, is always slow and silent —
Who else . . . is left behind?

Lord, there's so much to do — so little time —
teach us how to separate trash from treasure.
We pray that a modern vice might be converted and
return to
a life of virtue.
Let us pray for discrimination. Let us distinguish
between the work of the blessed and the work of the
busy-busy.
Let us discriminate, then begin to eliminate.

Friends, resist the temptation, don't look at your
watches —
let go of time
and allow the Beloved to lead you lovely into the
desert.
Not the Sinai or the Sahara
but into those quiet, empty spaces hidden in this
day —
desert spaces devoid of ticking clocks
and lethal deadlines.

Children of God —
let each of us find a sandpile, a little desert lot,
behind the garage or at the beginning of the day,
silent and strong
with the slow scent of sagebrush,
and there, as in our younger days —
the Divine Friend will speak —
not to our heads but to our hearts!

Free from haste and the violence of rushing,
we can do one thing, slowly, at a time.
Then we can respond as in the days of our youth —
with abundant affection,
     dedication,
          and dreams.

Coming forth from those empty spaces, desert-
places —
kissed by silence,
we shall be able to savor —
The Spirit Supreme,
sip by sip
in every, *every* segment of our lives.

A Prayer for Someone in a Hurry

Lord, help me this day
     to s l o w down.
It will not be easy for You — even You —
     to slow me down
     for I seem caught in the traffic-rush of life.
I rush through my prayers,
     hurry through my meals
     and run from one thing to another.
But I have faith
     that my choices and Your graces together
     can change my racetrack style of life.

I know, Lord, even before You whisper it in my ear,
    that You are waiting for me
    in the slower, quieter things of life.
Teach me, Lord of Life,
    how to eat my food with awareness;
    show me how to walk deliberately
    rather than constantly run,
    how to truly visit and be present
    rather than merely exchanging words.
Help me, Divine Friend,
    to take my time in praying to You.
Show me that it is good
    just to "waste" time with You in such acts
    as enjoying a sunset or a friendship.

With Your presence and assistance,
    I will attempt to do all things with mindfulness:
    slowly, carefully
    and fully aware of what I am doing.
Then, with Your grace, I shall find You, my God,
    in those unhurried and mindful moments.

Amen+ *(said very slowly)*

Simplicity and Prayer

Those who wish to pray always and all ways must also discover the importance of simple living. The function of simplicity is not penance but liberation. Prayer and simplicity are natural companions and nourish one another. But, in our modern age, the lack of a simple lifestyle is one of the reasons that we find it difficult to pray outside of "church" times. When our lives are complex, non-simple, and when they are devoid of prayer we will also find them to be lacking in nourishment for the inner person.

Today, both bread and toilet paper are so soft and squeezable. The bread section of your grocery store offers a variety of bread. Most of it is made from refined, bleached flour, filled with conditioners, artificial flavorings and preservatives. The ancient prophet Isaiah asks an excellent supermarket question: "Why spend your money for what is not bread; your wages for what fails to satisfy?" (Is 55: 1 - 3). Not only in health food stores but recently in most grocery stores natural whole grain breads are offered. On an increasing number of labels we are beginning to see the word "natural" and the statement "no artificial flavoring and preservatives." Recent style trends in fashion for both men and women reflect a desire for that which is more natural, simple, and comfortable. Is this movement toward simplicity and naturalism just another fad or is it a cultural movement that will have and is having an impact on history? Regardless of the answer, we cannot dismiss the fact that new lifestyles based on simplicity are becoming more common in our American society.

Simplicity can be viewed from at least four different approaches: first, a cultural approach that shows itself in architecture, food, fashions and in life patterns. It can also be approached, secondarily, as a sociopolitical, if not economic issue. The world is running out of certain major natural resources, and we of the Western world must learn to reduce our consumption. Americans, while being only six percent of the total world population, use fifty percent of the earth's raw materials to maintain a certain lifestyle. The ever-increasing cost of living has all of us searching for ways to save money, for simple and inexpensive ways of living. The third and ancient approach to simplicity is religious and is a virtue called "holy poverty." The purpose of this approach is not to "save money" but rather to save one's soul! Inner poverty, an un-possessed heart, is a means to mystical union with God. The final and fourth approach to simplicity is suggested by the question of Isaiah, "Why spend your hard-earned money on what fails to give you satisfaction?" Is a simple life important not only for prayer and economics, but also to find satisfaction for the different hungers of the human heart?

These four possible approaches are not divided but united as one. They are like four cords woven into a rope, forming a cultural-political-mystical-satisfying way of life. Let us now examine simplicity in the light of the search for satisfaction. Daily, we are told by the multitude of media about a thousand-and-one objects, which if purchased, will bring us satisfaction. But do they make us satisfied? What about the needs of others, especially those on the other side of the earth? Are their needs of any concern to us?

Within the last century, the rapid advances of technology have allowed us (that is some of us, about six percent of the earth's family) to use raw materials and resources at a rate never seen before. Technology has given us the ability to waste food, energy and resources while a social attitude asks the question "Why not?" We, as Americans, are not by nature more exploitative than those who have lived in previous ages. They, unlike us, simply lacked the technology and modern means that make it so easy to be so. Consumption is so effortless it becomes unconscious. We don't think about waste as unethical or anti-natural as we consume large amounts of resources.

John, the apostle and close friend of Jesus, said, "If a man has enough to live on, and yet when he sees his brother in need shuts up his heart against him, how can it be said that divine love dwells within him?" (1 John 3:17). Can we close our hearts and eyes to how we live, eat, dress or entertain ourselves and at the same time seek to be fully one with God? This makes a simple lifestyle a question of mysticism. Centuries before Christ, divine wisdom spoke through a holy book in China, the *Tao Te Ching*. The words of Christ about poverty and simplicity seem to no longer awaken the heart. Perhaps to reflect upon another tradition will help us hear again the Gospel. In the 77th chapter of this holy book of China we read, "The Way of heaven is to take from those who have too much and give to those who do not have enough. Man's way is different. He takes from those who do not have enough to give to those who already have too much. What man has more than enough and gives it to the world? Only the man of the Way." Can we continue to fill our closets with more and more clothing, our basements with more and more unused possessions and still call ourselves the people of the Way and friends of Him who called Himself *the Way*?

According to the World Wildlife Fund, the average American eats thirty percent more food than is needed for normal living. The next time we empty our dinner plates into the garbage, we can also reflect on these words from the 53rd chapter of the *Tao Te Ching:* "Some wear gorgeous clothing, carry sharp swords, and indulge themselves with food and drink; they have more possessions than they can use. They are robber barons." That we might be considered as robber barons or baronesses is a hard fact to face. A greater tragedy is that all this consumption of food and energy doesn't give us satisfaction and happiness. As Isaiah might have asked: "Why do you use up fifty percent of the world's resources for what fails to satisfy you?"

Simplicity that leads to satisfaction in life is concerned not with merely the number of possessions, but includes a concern for our use of time, our priorities, our diet, the care of our bodies, our work, and recreation. As a result, simplicity should be approached as a total lifestyle. To live such a simple lifestyle is extremely difficult, as religious orders and communities, whose members are vowed to poverty, can all testify!

The consumer consumption of more and more objects is what keeps our American economic system in operation. Can we then find an American spirituality without being a constant consumer of unnecessary objects? We are given the promise that these purchased objects will give us satisfaction or our money will be cheerfully refunded. But we don't find satisfaction or find our money being refunded! When our day is complicated with consumption instead of simply with satisfiers, it is no wonder we don't feel like praying or doing anything "natural." In the third century before Christ, a Chinese holy man named Chuang Tzu stated it well when he wrote, "He who seeks to extend his control is nothing but an operator . . . When he tries to extend his power over objects, those objects gain control over him. He who is controlled by objects loses possession of his inner self; if he no longer values himself, how can he value others? If he no longer values others, he is abandoned. He has nothing left!" Prayer is a natural action for those in possession of their inner selves and not "possessed" by objects. True prayer gives satisfaction because it is an experience of the presence of God in our hearts. Besides prayer and meditation, what else can give us satisfaction and is an experience of God?

The answer to this question is found in a reflection upon one of the modern inventions of the past century, the photographic camera. The camera (with its product, the photograph) is an evolutionary invention because it allows a human function, the memory, to be expanded. Memory has the tendency to fade or become distorted with time. For example, have you ever returned to your childhood home or school and been amazed at how much smaller it looked than your memory had pictured it? The camera, as an extension of the human memory, never forgets or distorts the historical image it has made. The camera has the possibility to record the image of just about anything: objects large and small, people and events. Now, keeping in mind that the camera can allow us to remember what is important and valuable, perhaps it can tell us what is important to us. Take out your family photo album. Will not nine out of ten photos be pictures of people? Is it not people that are valuable and not things? Our family, our friends, those with whom we share our lives and our hearts; it is these who we wish to remember with the memory-machine, the camera. Can you imagine a family photo album filled with snapshots of TV sets, cars, rings, stacks of money, stocks and bonds, racks of clothing? With our camera, we "remember" the satisfying and important human experiences like marriages, baptisms, vacations, and get-togethers. People and the celebrations that happen when people come together are what fill our hearts as at a banquet.

A simple lifestyle is one that places prime value on those human relationships. Such a life simplifies our activities and our desires so we can find satisfaction in loving others and in being loved. "No one has ever seen God," said St. John, "yet, if we love one another, God dwells in us, and His love is brought to perfection in us" (1 John 4:12). A simple lifestyle should proclaim that it is people that are primary and not property, that it is persons and not institutions that are important, that it is friends and not finances that bring us not only satisfaction but the perfection of God's love in us as well. In the loving of God and each other we meet at the very center of mysticism. If we wish to begin to live such a satisfying lifestyle, where do we begin?

We could begin by dropping a favorite American word: "super." Super means great, large, powerful, big and independent. In place of super we must begin to use words like simple, small, little, and interdependent. We need a new type of hero: not a superman or even a superwoman, but simplemen and simplewomen. We need a new breed of heroic people who aspire not to climb the highest mountain or become millionaires overnight, but rather those who can live in harmony with creation and with all people on this planet Earth, who by lives of simplicity can show us how to live with technology without losing touch with our inner selves. These persons will be political mystics whose lives, filled with satisfaction and the Spirit, will heal the world. Where or how do we begin? Anywhere, as long as it is somewhere! The wisdom of ancient India spoke of the "how" of such a work: "By degrees the wise man should free himself of unwholesome habits; also by degrees he should develop wholesome ones . . ." (Charak Samhita). Let any efforts of reform be gradual and in harmony with the rest of our lives. We could begin by looking in our closets, basements and attics and asking a simple question, "Do I really need this? Am I a robber baron if I store away what another might be able to use?" We can begin by looking at our diets and our eating habits and asking, "Do I eat thirty percent more food than I really need? Do I eat healthy foods and eat that food in a mindful manner?" As we examine our life patterns we might ask other questions: "Do I show reverence to my body by proper exercise, re-creation and leisure? Is my life simple enough to allow time for friends, family and time just to have fun? Is my life free of excessive activities so as to allow me proper time for prayer, reading, medi-tation and reflection?" We cannot realistically expect any growth without setting aside some time daily for meditation and silence. Finally, "Can I refrain from judging others concerning possessions and also re-fuse to judge myself?" Instead of judging, let us channel our time into the creation of a lifestyle that will bring satisfaction as well as a seat in heaven.

Since we learn more from stories than from stud-ies, allow me to close with an old legend from Europe told by the Brothers Grimm. Once upon a time, a poor pious peasant died and went to heaven. At the same time, a rich man also arrived at the gates of

111

heaven. Saint Peter came out and warmly welcomed the rich man and took him into heaven, apparently not seeing the poor peasant standing there as well. As soon as the gates shut, all kinds of rejoicing began inside. The poor man standing outside could hear music, loud singing and great rejoicing inside heaven. After awhile, all was quiet again; in fact, very, very quiet. The gates of heaven opened and Saint Peter came out and ushered in the poor man. The peasant was all ready for the grand singing and music, but there was none! Oh, he was received with great affection by both the saints and angels, but not with the grand reception given to the man of wealth and power. The poor peasant turned to Saint Peter and said, "I had hoped that heaven would have been different than earth. Down there, the rich and powerful are treated with honor and special privileges both in the cathedral and in the town square, while the poor man is overlooked. Why is it that even here in God's house partiality to the rich is shown?" Saint Peter, putting his arm around the poor man said, "By no means, my holy brother. You are just as dear to us as anyone else and you will enjoy every heavenly delight that the rich man will have, and more. Your heart will be filled with satisfaction. But, you see, poor people like yourself come to heaven every hour. A rich man, like that one . . . well, they do not come more than once every hundred years!"

A Prayer for Simplicity

Lord of True Liberty,
>You who commissioned Moses
>to lead Your chosen children from bondage in Egypt
>to the freedom of a new land,
>help me to find a real freedom in simplicity.

Cure me, Lord, of "buyer's itch";
>heal me of the consumer's consumption
>that keeps me constantly discontent
>and continuously craving more and more.

Show to me the joys of a simple lifestyle
>whereby in my "freedom from things"
>I shall have more time and energy
>to invest in my relationships with those I love,
>with myself, and with You, my God.

Help me, by the example of Your Son, Jesus,
>to place my value in those things
>that neither moth nor thief can take from me.

And, as I strive for greater simplicity —
>in my prayers, my lifestyle, my desires —
>I shall find greater happiness in life itself.

May my efforts at simplicity not cease
>with looking into my closet and counting clothes,
>but may they take on their greatest energy and zeal
>when looking into my heart
>and removing all that is not in the fashion
>of Your divine heart,
>all that blocks my loving others.

May I be reminded frequently that whatever form
    my attempts at simplicity may take
    that it is a simple heart
    which You first and foremost desire.

I ask this, Lord, through the intercession
    of Your Son, Jesus the Christ,
    who lives with You and the Holy Spirit,
    now and forever.

Amen+

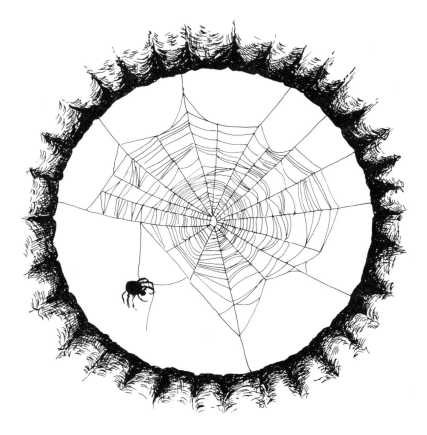

Patience and Prayer

Fact: "There are no clocks in Las Vegas gambling casinos." At least, so it seems, no clocks are placed where the gamblers may see them; the reason being that "watching the clock" hampers the skill of a good gambler. Since waiting is essential to winning, patience is the archvirtue of gamblers . . . and of people who like to fish.

Patience is a necessary daily ingredient for life as well as for prayer. "She has the patience of a saint," is a common expression that reveals that the possession of this virtue is one of the "signs" of holiness. As a quality of the heart, this ability "to wait" seems to be a feminine grace! Patience is the ability to "suffer time." The word comes from a Greek mother word which means to suffer. Our English word, patient, meaning someone being treated by a doctor, also comes from this same Greek root word. Patience is a feminine virtue because from studies of human behavior it seems that women, more than men, are capable of enduring long periods of suffering and pain without breaking under the strain. Since women must bear the nine months of pregnancy, suffering physical and emotional stress, they have

117

been gifted by God with this beautiful ability to suffer time. While we may call the virtue feminine, women lack this quality of being patient just as easily as men!

We are all intended to be a balance of masculine and feminine qualities. The purpose of holiness is wholeness. The balance of the two sides of human nature, the gentle and the strong, the dark and the light, the masculine and the feminine, is part of the ongoing work of the inner journey. Patience is one test of the degree of a person's inner (or spiritual) balance. In each of our lives we have need of this ability to wait. We seem to want everything RIGHT NOW! What is it that we want RIGHT NOW? We want things like love, success, happiness, social justice, equality, reform, our suit cleaned and pressed, our hair dried, our rice cooked and our meals ready to eat . . . and at least 10,000 other things right now.

We also want the Kingdom of God RIGHT NOW! We read in the Gospels that "the Kingdom is at hand!" and yet we see little evidence of its presence in our world. We wait, bearing the slowness of God's redemption. We suffer the slowness of our human evolution, the conversion of the human heart. All around us we see war, greed, disregard for persons, oppression of the poor and countless other evils alive and well after two thousand years of "redemption." We hate to wait on God. The potent promise given to our great spiritual grandfather, Abraham, demanded waiting not just a few years, but waiting for thousands. Scripture and even fairy tales are full of instructions on the art of waiting. The story of the three little pigs building their houses shows the virtue of taking one's time to build a good, solid house. If you "suffer" patience now, you will not have to suffer in the future as did the two little pigs who couldn't wait.

The very act of waiting, the peaceful suffering of time, is prayer. Part of the discipline of prayer is that of patience. We must learn how to suffer the slow growth of inner stillness by daily sitting still. We must suffer the slow conversion of the heart as it is organically reformed. We must patiently return, day after day, week after week, to the discipline of daily prayer without the reward of seeing instant results of that time spent in prayer. The lack of patience is one of the reasons why prayer is abandoned by most people . . . they are unable to wait long enough to experience the fruits of their time in silence. Without patience there can be no real prayer! Oh, we can have prayers, the saying of prayers, but we will not have the "spirit" of prayer without the art of learning how to wait. Prayer is patient waiting. The prayer of meditation, especially, is an adventure open only to those who have cultivated that feminine grace of patience.

We can learn a lesson from the little spider. Watch a spider as she patiently rebuilds her web each time it is broken or removed. Seldom will she move its location but chooses to rebuild it with patience. She reweaves its broken strands each time they are broken. She waits, in patience, for dinner to come into her white cosmos of tiny threads. Daily, we weave webs of worship as we connect the countless threads of our lives which are held together by a divine center. We finish our prayers and we are peaceful. We are at one with God and with each other, when suddenly our webs are broken by a variety of possibilities: a failure, some thoughtless mistake, sickness, or some misunderstanding with a person we love.

Like the spider, we must return again and again to rebuild our webs by bringing together the threads of our lives and uniting them to the divine center within. Without such work, our lives become disconnected, unpeaceful and broken. Perhaps the next time we see a spider's web, we can see it as a spiritual classroom and not simply something to be swept away. While the spider is not among our religious symbols, it is one for the American Indians. The Hopi Tribe of the Southwest has in its holy books a holy woman. She is the Divine Mother, but her name isn't Mary, it is Spider Woman. She brings together the idea of patience and the Holy Mother as intercessor between God and the people.

As spider-like patience is essential to prayer, so prayer is essential to life. Prayer — true prayer — never lives in isolation. For those persons who understand its meaning, it is not the hobby of the holy or a luxury in life; it holds the pattern for all life. Just as we reweave each day the elements of life in our prayer, so we must do the same in every one of our personal relationships. We need to constantly reweave the fabric of our marriages, our work, our lives that are so easily broken by a word, a deed, a habit, or the loss of enthusiasm. We need patience with each other; with the old, the young, the sick, the slow, and with God! Psalm 36 speaks of this last need, the need to wait on God: "Be still before the Lord and wait in patience." We must learn how to sit still, to stop being in a hurry, and wait for God to move within our lives. We still ourselves in prayer, aware that the graces we need, the special gifts we desire, will come to us when we are ready. Whatever is necessary for our spiritual journeys will come when the time is ready. Until that time we simply sit in stillness, waiting, and even seeing pleasure, finding fun, in waiting!

To have fun waiting, what a strange idea! Certainly it is not fun to wait for a long freight train to pass a crossing (especially on a hot summer day) or to have to wait an hour past our appointment time in some doctor's office. Having to wait on others, even to wait on God, is not fun. That's because we are in a hurry; to wait is to have *our* plans upset. But if God is life and the purpose of life is to find pleasure in God, then why can't there be fun in the action of waiting? Try it the next time you are called upon to wait for someone or something. Open up that gift of time and find the fun within.

In marriage, art, work, sports, and prayer, we must learn how to suffer the time of growth. This doing of nothing: isn't that just plain old back porch procrastination? Can't patience be seen as only the intentional putting off until tomorrow that which should be done today? Procrastination is a love affair with tomorrow, which is that golden day when we will change, pray more, read, fix the back door, play with the children or take our wife out to dinner. Procrastination is not a virtue; it is a form of being asleep. Patience is vigilant waiting, a waiting that is full, pregnant with dreams, hopes, ideas and with peace. Such a waiting is not resignation, as when we resign ourselves to the fates. Patience is loving and dynamic surrender. In Islam, this type of patient surrender is expressed in the term "Inshallah" which means "God willing."

Such a surrender is possible when we have the awareness that our life is part of a cosmic interlocking system which is itself composed of complex countless other systems. Such patient waiting can be a consciousness that we are "not-in-control;" we are not a king or god. Patience is a sign that our needs (at this very moment) must be balanced with the needs and lives of others. Waiting for anyone or anything is a prayer of communion with the rest of the cosmos. As such, it is always a prayer of humility and truth. The truth is we are but a part of a much greater whole and not the sum total of all.

Nor is this art of fruitful waiting to be confused with stoicism. Our non-anxious waiting for God to

121

act or for the plumber to finish his job is not the repressed emotion of the stoic. Stoicism is that indifference to pain or pleasure that has been, at various times in history, valued as a virtue. Something more than the repression of strong feelings without any external sign of distress is prescribed for those seeking a *wholistic* holiness.

Waiting for our dreams to come true, for someone to grow up, for the "right" person to fall in love with us, is the waiting of an expectant mother. This sort of waiting is not a passive acceptance of delay, but rather active, dynamic waiting. This form of patience is filled with the eagerness of a coming encounter between the dream in the womb and the mother who carries the dream. In our lives we wait for such living encounters whenever we continue to work for justice or peace, without losing our hope or our excitement with the dream. The kingdom of God comes slowly. We must carry the dreams in our hearts, feed them with prayer each day, as we patiently transform the grubby realities of our lives into the stuff of eternity.

God, so it seems, is a gynecologist. We are all patients in the waiting room of the world. We thumb through old, dog-eared magazines and wait. We feel the mystery of life stirring within us, but we are tired of waiting. In the anxiousness of our impatience we look to see what time it is, only to discover that in God's waiting room, as in Caesar's Palace in Vegas . . . that's right, there are no clocks!

A Prayer for Waiting

Lord, my God,
   though I am confident that You hear my prayers
   and that You fulfill all my needs,
   I find the need for You to teach me
   the holy art of patience.
I hate to wait
   and am in a hurry even now as I pray to You.
I am in a hurry to learn how to pray,
   in a hurry to become holy,
   in a hurry to do Your will.

Reveal to me that Your time is eternal
   and that in Your good time You will answer
   our every prayer for peace and justice.
Meanwhile, may Your delightful creature, the turtle,
   be a symbol of my journey to You
   who are my divine source and reward.
Let me stop my anxious rushing and follow his lead —
   making my way, slow but sure,
   day by day, prayer by prayer,
   kind deed followed by attentive, kind deed,
   toward You, my God.
Surprise me with the reward
   that if I can be patient with myself
   and the seeming slowness of my unfolding
   I shall find that it is much easier
   to be patient and loving with others.

Finally, Lord, I thank You
   for Your patience with me over all these years.

I am grateful that You allow
my shortcomings and imperfections
to slowly drop off
and have virtues just as surely take their place.
Share with me, my Lord,
Your divine and enduring patience.
I ask this in the name of Your Son, Jesus,
who lives with You and the Holy Spirit.

Amen+

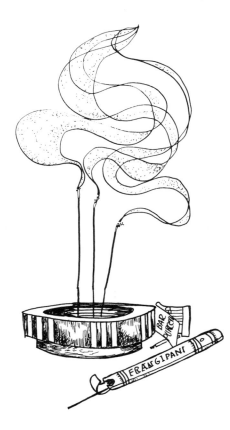

Discipline —
To Feast or Fast?

"Would you pass the salt, please?" This is a request so common that it is heard daily at almost every table in the land. Salt is essential not only to the cooking of our food, but to adding that "special" touch of flavor before we eat. Salt is essential to our bodies and to life itself. Of His disciples, Jesus said, "You are the salt of the earth; you are to heighten the flavor of life around you" (Mt 5:13). To be a disciple of His is to be the salt of life, and that is a vital and responsible vocation. Being salt is for all of us the primal vocation. The spiritual vitality (the saltiness) of our lives is not a permanent inner-quality. This inner-quality can fade, be lost, and when we lose its special quality, we lose the flavor of our existence.

Spiritual discipline . . . an unpleasant, even bitter, term. Like a hefty drink of salt water, we find that spiritual discipline is unpleasant and undesirable. We prefer to flow "with the spirit" and pray, fast, and perform other such disciplines when we are inspired. Just as too much salt in our soup can make that soup so undesirable that we push the bowl away, so too much discipline or the wrong type causes us to push away the bowl of religion. Several years ago the Church discarded her laws on mandatory fast and abstinence from meat on certain days. This repeal of an imposed regulation of spiritual discipline was met by many with a sigh of relief. For countless people it signaled the abandonment of spiritual discipline from their daily lives instead of the voluntary selection of a personal discipline. The result for many people was like finding oneself on a salt-free diet. Anyone who has ever had to be on a salt-free diet knows how flat and tasteless food becomes. We lack a truly good substitute for salt. Daily life without some form of spiritual discipline will eventually become equally as flat and tasteless.

All the truly great religions of this earth have always had their spiritual disciplines. These may vary in their form, but they are the same in their purpose. The primal purpose of any spiritual discipline is to be an instrument, an avenue, by which we experience God! The goal of spiritual self-discipline is mysticism. From the variety of spiritual disciplines, we could mention prayers, fasting, chanting, dancing, pilgrimages, vigils, reading and yoga. You will notice that penance is not mentioned in this list. We could ask, "Are these not forms of asceticism and penance, as well as spiritual discipline?"

Penance and asceticism are not proper forms of spiritual discipline since their purpose is different. Penance is a religious action of voluntary suffering, as a sign of personal sorrow for sin. Penance is a reaction to the haunting fear that God is not satisfied with an honest expression of sorrow, but demands restitution for sins. Penances, as forms of denial of the things we enjoy, are self-inflicted penalties whose purpose is to help your case when you appear before the divine judge. They were types of early religious plea bargaining meant to lighten your eternal sen-

128

tence. Asceticism is a Greek word that refers to the exercise performed by a spiritual athlete. Historically, this form of religious discipline has had more to do with the rejection of the body than with the experience of God. Asceticism has been tainted with the belief that the body is an obstacle to holiness and must be forced into submission. If you wish to experience God, you then must deny the earthly so as to be un-earthly and therefore heavenly. In such an outlook, the good life (feasting, drinking, and, we might add, marriage) is directly opposed to holiness. If you doubt this historical-spiritual approach, answer one simple question: how many married, canonized saints can you name?

Both "penitentialism" (the practicing of penance) and asceticism tend to focus the attention of persons upon themselves. By their very nature, they are self-concerning and ego-building. As a spiritual athlete, the ascetic, who neither drinks nor enjoys the pleasures of the body, is highly prized because he or she proclaims the victory of the will over the lower passions and needs of the human body. As we examine the pages of the Gospel, we find that Jesus did not promote asceticism. He, likewise, did not promote penance for sins. When He forgave sinners, their sins were forgiven and He did not require penitential restitution. Like Moses, He also did not require fasting from His disciples. This omission is extremely interesting and raises the question about what sorts of spiritual discipline He did promote.

While not denying the value of fasting, Jesus simply did not ask His disciples to fast. His enemies raised this very question when they said to Him, "John's disciples are always fasting and saying prayers, and the disciples of the Pharisees too, but Yours go on eating and drinking . . ." (Lk 5:33). The disciples were followers of Jesus and perhaps that is

129

the reason they did not fast. The lifestyle of Jesus, unlike that of John the Baptist, was not one of asceticism, or at least so it seems. Speaking of Himself, Jesus said, "For John the Baptist comes not eating bread, not drinking wine and you say, 'he is possessed.' The Son of Man comes eating and drinking, and you say, 'Look, a glutton and a drunkard . . . ' " (Lk 7:33).

The spiritual discipline of Jesus, the Jesus-yoga, seems to draw people closer to feasting instead of the classical ascetical practice of fasting from feasting. The Gospel stories are spun around supper tables, wedding feasts, the multiplication of bread and wine, and with dinners surrounded by saints and sinners. When referring to the next life, heaven, He speaks of banquets, choice wine, wedding feasts, and rejoicing. Jesus, as a spiritual master, is uniquely the master of the feasting table. He calls Himself bread and says that eternal life is dependent upon eating and drinking His Body and Blood. His appearances after the resurrection center about eating with His apostles. Finally, it was at a meal, at a supper table, that He gave to His followers His greatest sacrament, the Eucharistic Communion Meal. This dinner-time worship would become the central mystery of His kingdom. At that same supper table, He urged the adoption of His greatest spiritual discipline (the yoga of Jesus) when He washed their feet and told them to imitate this discipline in their own lives. This was the yoga of service to others, even in the most humble of tasks, and it was to be a doorway to experiencing God.

This spiritual discipline of service is a form of fasting. It is a fasting that finds its expression in visiting those in jail, feeding the hungry, caring for the sick, washing dishes, chopping wood, sharing clothing, or even offering a bed. These are the new yoga of a new kingdom. This is not a fasting with the mouth, but with the heart. It is the emptying of self and self-concern, as we focus our attention not upon ourselves, but upon others and their needs. The prophet Isaiah (58:5) had stated that God desires not the fasting from food or the wearing of sackcloth, but rather that you share your bread with those in need and release those who are bound. This form of discipline calls for an emptiness of our self-concern and the end of that vicious self-preoccupation. The discipline of service, symbolized by the foot washing, is indeed the raja yoga, the royal yoga of Jesus.

The paradox is that while seeming to be easier, this form of fasting, which is the fasting of the heart, is far more difficult than any fasting of the body. To fast once a week has numerous benefits for both body and spirit. More and more medical persons are encouraging such a practice. We know that historically, fasting was a part of all religious pathways. Jesus does not prohibit this discipline, and for those who practice it He advises simply that it be done naturally and without any fuss. He does, however, promote fasting of the heart: "If you wish to be My disciple, you must deny your very self" (Lk 9:23).

We might well reflect on how we can fast with our hearts as we feast together. Since the mystery of the Kingdom seems to center around the table, this reflection could be a positive value to us. As disciples of Jesus, we could be called "the disciples of the table." With a certain freedom we could put these words into our Lord's mouth: "By this will all know that you are My disciples, by the way you eat and drink together!"

Is it possible that we could bring to eating a new and higher consciousness? Are not breakfast, lunch, and dinner also times of prayer and communion? How can we learn to have these daily times become something more than times of biological feeding?

We can learn to fast in the heart as we learn to fast from "fast" food. Since we are all busy people, living busy lives, we are constantly seeking new ways to save time. We can fast from eating-on-the-run, from an absent-mindedness of the taste and smell of our food. We can fast from "speed" eating, and instead take our time to be present to the great mystery that is present on our plates. Of the Pueblo Indians of New Mexico it was said, "Our people eat quietly, gently, recognizing with inner feelings that the corn or squash were at one time growing, cared for, and each plant alive. Now they are prepared to become part of us, part of our bodies and our minds. The food is very sacred."

We can learn to fast from "junk food." As we become aware of the sacredness of our bodies, we will treat them with reverence and seek to fill them with life instead of with chemicals. Good food and wholesome food requires time and also money, for that which is quick and cheap is often also destructive. Time and money spent on meals should be entered in the budget under prayer and worship, if we are truly disciples of the table. While eating we can learn to fast from discussing unpleasant topics, from arguments and disagreements. We can refuse to let the dining table become a conference table for business or a courtroom for the passing of judgments on others. We can remember that half of every meal is the feast of sharing stories, laughter, and the history of the day.

We can also learn to fast from routine by fasting from *not* praying before we eat. The purpose of prayers before a meal is not to bless the food (it has been already blessed by sun, rain, and earth and is filled with Life = God); the purpose is to lift up our hearts. Before we begin this act, we raise our hearts and consciousness to what it is we are about to perform. Meal prayers need not be solemn, pontifical invocations, but rather they need be only sincere and natural. A piece of bread, a cracker, broken and shared together in silence is perhaps one of the most powerful meal prayers. Henry Thoreau, writing in *Walden,* said, "Who has not sometimes derived an inexpressible satisfaction from his food in which appetite had no share? I have been thrilled to think that I owed a mental perception to the commonly gross sense of taste, that I have been inspired through the palate, that some berries which I had eaten on a hillside had fed my genius. 'The soul not being a mistress of herself,' says Thseng-tseu, 'one looks, and one does not see; one listens, and does not hear; one eats and one does not know the savor of food.' He who distinguishes the true savor of his food can never be a glutton; he who does not, cannot be otherwise. A puritan may go to his brown-bread crust with as gross an appetite as ever an alderman to his turtle." Meal prayers are but a means to help us taste and savor the Creator who is mystically present in His creation. A story is told about an anxious mother who came to see an old and holy priest with a problem. Her small son, after making his first Holy Communion, had complained to her that "God tasted just like bread!" She was anxious about what to say to her small son. The old priest asked her, "Is the problem that God tastes like bread or is it that bread tastes like God?"

Whether eating at home or away, we can learn to fast from ingratitude. Feasts do not walk to the table by themselves. Rather they demand energy, time, and creativity, if not ingenuity in these days of high food prices. The proper prayer response is that of *daily* gratitude and appreciation to the person who is responsible for the meal. Meals do not walk away from the table by themselves any more than pots and pans take showers. Part of the sharing of the sacred act of eating is the sharing of the cleaning and returning to their proper place the ceremonial objects of the feast: spoons, plates, and cups. The yoga of drying dishes can be filled with grace and mysticism!

These are but a few ways by which we can fast with our hearts as we feast together. Each home, each community should seek its own creative ways of fasting in the heart. Such fasting will season our lives with zest and affection.

While gratitude is a prayerful response, it is also one that is frequently forgotten in life. If we are salt, this will not be a problem. When was the last time you thanked a salt shaker for the richness it gave to your meal? We think about salt only when it is absent. So a true disciple, who is salt, will frequently not be appreciated for adding that special zest to life. We do not taste the salt in a correctly seasoned food, for the salt has that magical quality to bring out not its own flavor but the hidden flavor of the food. The true disciple is as inconspicuous as salt on a steak, but powerful in his or her spiritual mission in life. The real saint proclaims the taste of God in all of life, and not the taste of the saint!

Home and eating go together like apple pie and cheese. Every home has its sacred shrine: the family table. Every day has its communal prayer times: meal times! Over the centuries we have forgotten that theological truth, and, as a result, our family shrines have fallen into disrepair. Now is the time to season our tables with the sense of the holy. A drugstore counter, a table in a mansion or in a mobile home, even a brown paper sack, can all once again become the meeting place where we and God come together. At that mundane but mystical intersection, we can experience the living reality of a God who said, "I am the Bread of Life" (Jn 6:35). When we have

comprehended that simple sentence — God is Bread —
then we will have become Salt!

A Prayer for the Daily Gift of Bread

In a gloria of gratitude,
   I am made mindful of the many marvels of life
   that spark my heart.
You have not only given me life
   but continue to increase that life by nourishing me.
Blessed are You, Holy Sustainer,
   for the marvel of food,
   for bread and wine,
   for banquets and dinners, picnics and suppers.

With compassionate care
   You fed Moses and his people in the desert,
   and You sustain me, now, with daily manna
   at breakfast, lunch and dinner.

I am thankful for Your Son, Jesus,
   who was the living bread,
   broken, shared and eaten in love.
For that Holy Bread
   who calls me to share myself unselfishly
   as food for others,
   I bless You, Divine Source.

I take delight
  with Moses, Jesus, and all the holy ones,
  that parents, friends, teachers and poets,
  artists, musicians and people of prayer,
  have all been food for me.

Blessed are You, Boundless Father,
  who have shared with me the secret of life:
  to become nourishment and life for others.
May each meal I eat
  be a wonder of worship of You.

Blessed are You, Lord my God,
  who daily gives me bread to eat.

Amen+

Feasting as Prayer

In the last chapter we spoke of the relationship between prayer and our daily meals. Breakfast, lunch and dinner are indeed "prayer times." But beyond these daily devotions of eating, we, at special times, gather to celebrate and to feast. Feasting is natural to humans. It is an enjoyable and most ancient way of celebrating victories, weddings, anniversaries and the great feast days. Because these "feast" days are so enjoyable, we easily forget that they are also part of our art of praying all ways. Birthdays, Christmas, Easter, Thanksgiving, and all other "special" occasions are times of intimate communion with our Lord, who called Himself our food and drink. Feasting is an important part of the Christian life. Sharing food and drink is not only fun, it is also one of the most ancient of all prayers. To feast was to worship; and the way in which people looked upon eating is an insight into their sense of values.

In his Gospel, Mark tells us that the crowds were coming and going in such numbers that it was impossible for Jesus and His friends to eat! At this Jesus reacts and says, "Let's get out of here and go to some out-of-the-way place and rest a little" (Mk

6:31). Crowds were not new to the prophetic healer from Nazareth. With compassion He healed the sick, freed the possessed of demons and forgave their sins, but this was the last straw — to prevent Him and His friends from eating a meal! This reaction of Jesus and His friends to being hassled while they ate gives us an insight into another culture and what it valued. Feasting together, even the most common of meals, was a special time, sacred and symbolic. For the ancient peoples, eating and drinking together was filled with importance beyond simply "refueling" the body.

If one theme is central and constantly present in our Judaic-Christian religious tradition, that theme has to be eating! The story begins with Adam and Eve eating some food that they had been forbidden to eat. Then there is Abraham's feast for his three strangers who are angelic or divine figures, Moses and the dinner of the lamb that is known as the Passover Meal, God's daily feeding of the Jews in the desert with manna, and Isaiah's prophecy of eternity as a mountain-top, dripping with juicy foods and choice wines. The Gospels continued this love affair with eating. Jesus' favorite image of heaven is a banquet together at God's table. He refers to Himself as bread, drink, as food that grants eternal life. Some of the more beautiful scenes of His life are times of meal celebrations — at wedding dinners or at a friend's table — and His final meal becomes the occasion of the most important Christian sacrament, the Holy Eucharist. Even after His resurrection, we find Him eating with His disciples and appearing to them at dinner time. Indeed, for us, eating has deep religious and social significance. Or rather it did have that significance at one time, but perhaps not any longer!

Few "real" feasts remain. Feasts that are fun to prepare and fun to share with friends and family can be counted on the fingers of one hand. Christmas,

Thanksgiving, and sometimes Easter are times of great joy where the act of eating is an important aspect of the celebration of the feast. The rest of the time we usually eat "on the run" as we "grab a bite to eat," rushing off to a meeting, a movie, or back to work. We are a people eager for fast and easily prepared food because we are so busy. Our lives move at the same frantic beat as a hard rock song. Short of time, we hate to be bothered with cooking and preparing a meal, with setting a beautiful table or with drying dishes together.

McDonald's and all the rest of the roadside fast-food shops would have been beyond the imagination of ancient peoples . . . beyond imagination not because of the architecture, nor the technology of electronically-packaged and sanitary-sacked food, but simply beyond the idea of "fast-food!" The ancient ones would have been unable to comprehend why anyone would want to rush through the ritual of eating. "Fast-food" would have been as inconceivable to them as "fast-love!" The last century has been the "century of machines." Machines have changed our cultural patterns and values significantly. Machines don't eat, don't take time for a leisurely meal; they are simply refueled or plugged in! We have patterned our lives upon these machines in childlike admiration of their power and efficiency.

Few societies in our 20th century could have such an array of time-saving machines and such a bountiful supply of food. Yet, it is our society that has given birth to "eating-on-the-run." In an industrial society, a capitalistic one, time is money, and so eating easily becomes a waste of time and money. A secret desire may be lurking in our 20th century hearts — to do away with meals! We could be fed by plastic tubes injected into our arms or nourished by a handful of pills, and then off to our work or to our favorite event. Such intravenous feeding would eliminate the problem of dirty dishes and messy pans, not to mention the trouble of setting the table. So, freed of dish-washing and having to prepare a meal, life would become "heavenly." Some twenty years ago when I was a young assistant priest, we had a Jesuit priest who came to help at the parish one weekend. I offered him breakfast and he surprised me by saying, "No thanks, that's too much bother. I've found an easier way." He then took two eggs, cracked them open, tilted his head back and consumed them raw in a split second. He smiled and walked out the door to help with Communion in the church. Who knows, perhaps the Jesuits are secretly behind the fast-food franchises.

As we frantically rush into the 21st century, not even twenty years away, we hunger for authentic spiritual experiences. We seek religious experiences that are not pseudo-pious, phony, unreal or embalmed with dusty dogma. We seek religious expressions or worship that have their roots in the ancient rituals and myths but are, at the same time, part of us in all our modern manners. Perhaps the place to begin to find these spiritual experiences is at our next meal.

And maybe the ancient memory of feasting isn't completely dead. Indeed, we know that last year cookbooks led the parade of the top best sellers across our nation. Perhaps we can recall and revive the primitive joys of eating and drinking together. And, by doing so, find in this most basic of all human activities what our ancestors found in it: a sense of the sacred. Each Sunday we come together to celebrate the Christian agape, the meal of love. Even with the radical changes of the past fifteen years in worship, the Sacred Meal has problems resembling a meal. Whether it is due to this lack of resemblance or to the powerful influence of our industrial society, we have failed to carry home from Church the message that all meals are mystical.

We have forgotten that our Lord promised to be with us in the "breaking of the bread," let alone in the broken bread of daily meals. If you read between the lines of the Gospel books, you can see how they are also cookbooks and how our Lord's disciples may truly be recognized by "the way they *feast* together." Christian homes, then, should be recognized immediately by the importance that is placed in such areas as the kitchen, the dining room table, and, of course, the wine cellar!

Speed, our constant state of being in a hurry, is one cause for the loss of a sense of graciousness and manners. Rarely do we now find the ritual and beauty that once surrounded eating, since these things take time. Unless we are willing to take time, we will never be able to experience the mystic pleasures of eating and drinking together. Without that daily experience, our sacred meals also become just another expression of "fast-food!"

To feast doesn't require a lot of money, but rather imagination and love. As Friedrich Nietzsche said, "The trick is not to arrange a festival but to find people who can enjoy it." A feast requires only simple things such as people who love one another (as small a number as two), some food and drink and a sense of magic. That happens when we come together to share food, life stories, tales, jokes and laughter. For eating is communion. Eating as prayer, as an essential part of our spiritual lives, would not be that difficult to discover again. With the proper attitude and a willingness to take the time required, we would soon be conscious that meal time is a sacred time. If we were to introduce some ritual once again into our meals, we might enjoy them more and

143

find them to be more than biologically nourishing. Some simple ritual at the beginning of meals is needed — prayer, silence, a toast, the breaking of a piece of bread — something that will touch our consciousness of the sacred nature of the gift before us.

If we are looking for some spiritual experience in our daily lives, the place to begin is our next meal. The way to begin is to be aware that dinner time is holy time. Alexander Dumas, not the famous writer but a famous cook, insisted that certain wines should only be drunk kneeling, with the head bared. Perhaps, if we truly understood the sacredness of feasting, not only certain wines, but all food and drink would be consumed in that holy position.

A Prayer for Feasting

For those who love You, O Lord,
    is not everything holy, everything prayerful?
As I prepare to celebrate any feast,
    give delight to my heart and arouse my taste buds.
May I truly realize that happy are those times
    when we can pause in the midst of our labors
    and share good food and drink,
    joyful song and story with one another.

From the first day of creation,
    Your children worshipped You
    in the act of eating and drinking together,
    and beheld therein Your divine presence.

Each feast is meant to be a taste
 of that eternal celebration at Your table
 in the cosmic feasting hall.

I thank You, Lord of the Feast,
 for holidays and holy days,
 for anniversaries and victory celebrations,
 for homecomings and weddings,
 for all these times and many more
 when we can pray with food and drink,
 in the company of candles and conversation.

I thank You, my God,
 that in the holy feast of Passover
 and especially in the Last Supper of Your Son, Jesus,
 You gave to us holy signs
 of Your eternal presence at our tables
 and a promise of the great feast
 that awaits us in the life to come.
May every feast in which I share,
 be praise, honor and glory
 to You, my Lord and my God.

Amen+

The Prayer of Napping

As we search for a spirituality in which we can pray in all ways and always and which reflects our national, local and even global lives, it is important that we realize the difference between Prayer and prayers. Prayer is a way of life in which we are always facing the Mystery, while prayers can take many forms within that way of living. An example of the difference between prayers and Prayer is found in the fourth chapter of St. Mark's Gospel (Mk 4:38-41). Here, Mark presents an interesting and unusual form of prayer. Interesting and important for us who are Americans is the experience that we find there: Jesus engaged in the Prayer of Napping! It was late in the day, and leaving the crowds that had gathered around the small fishing boat from which He had been teaching, Jesus and His friends set sail for the opposite side of the lake. Tired and exhausted, Jesus fell asleep with His head on a cushion in the stern of the boat. A violent storm quickly came upon them and began to send spray and waves smashing over the sides of the small boat. His companions, filled with fear, awakened Him. They were unable to understand why He was asleep in the midst of possible death.

This Gospel adventure, filled with beautiful implications, is an ideal reading right after lunch on a hot afternoon, or for that matter, on any day. We, who so often feel guilty about napping, could do well to remember how the gentle rabbi had no trouble taking a nap in the midst of trouble. Not only naps, but coffee breaks, tea times, or just a plain old "take five" are sacramental and therefore times of prayer.

Persons on retreat often disclose that they find themselves sleeping during the day — mortal sin for busy messiahs out to redeem the world! These persons feel guilty about not using their time in a more productive way. Should not the spiritual life be pursued with the same organized sweat as all other work? Whether we are on a desert day (a day a month set aside for quiet and solitude) or on retreat or even in the midst of a normal day, we would do well to keep the memory of our Lord, as Mark said, "sound asleep" in the midst of turmoil.

Contemporary life seems to be a storm of activities that rages on all sides of us. There is so much work to do and so few people to do it and so little time in which it is to be done. Modern life with all its numerous inventions has allowed us to extend the frontiers of work. We have pushed back ancient limitations, but have not yet learned how to adjust to our new powers of the possible. The electric light has made it possible to work from pre-dawn darkness 'til midnight, or as in the case of some, all night long! As we surround ourselves with all sorts of machines (electric and otherwise), we begin to behave like machines. In former times, when the sun went down work had to stop. People had time to rest, talk, and tell stories. We, even with all our time-saving inventions, are like passengers in a small boat tossed about

148

by the storm of life and near to sinking. We long for the opposite shore of retirement and the dream of time to relax and taste life. But for now, row with all your might and work hard. When in the midst of all this busy activity we feel drowsy and are tempted to stop and rest, guilt and that inner taskmaster pounce upon us. When we fall asleep in our times of prayer or in meditation, we also feel guilty since we have so few precious minutes for prayer anyway.

As zealous Christians should we not be "on our toes," alert, awake and busy? For who wants to be caught napping, which is a sure sign of carelessness? But wasn't Jesus caught napping that afternoon on the lake? He was, to put it plainly, careless. To be careless is to be care-less, to be without care or anxiety. He was a casual and relaxed rabbi-teacher who was well aware that not He, but the Father was in control of the universe. That state of awareness is prayer. It is a way of facing the Mystery. Since God was in charge, why worry and be upset with undue care, for He and His friends were held in God's love which would shield them from all evil.

Our word "sleep" lends itself to this aspect of a natural care-less spirituality. Our word "sleep" comes from the German word "schlaff" which means "loose." To sleep, then, or to nap is to "hang loose," to be un-tight and to let go. Sleep at night or in short periods before bedtime is a beautiful expression of prayer since it is resting in God. It is letting go of our control of life. Sleep is a parable on prayer and it is also prayer. If we look only at the front side of sleep we might miss hidden implications. All things have a front and back door, and we should not be satisfied just to enter ideas from the front side only. The front door of sleep is bodily rest, but where does the back door lead?

The back door leads to the Prayer of Napping as
149

an external sacrament of the inner ability to "let go" of managing every aspect of our lives. It is an expression that we are able to allow the Divine Mystery to take over in the midst of troubles and deadlines. It is an expression of faith that the Divine Presence is even concerned with our seemingly common work and difficulties. Sleep is a form of humility for it says, "God is saving the world." To let go for coffee breaks or naps and to do so without guilt allows God a chance to save the world!

The "heresy of hurry-hurry" keeps knocking at the doors of our hearts with an ageless regularity. The H-H Heresy is the mistaken notion that God needs us to bring about the Kingdom, and without our rest-less efforts God will fail! The ancient psalm writer of Israel sang that "the Guardian of Israel never sleeps." Virtue, is to be God-like, and so we attempt to pattern our activities on that pattern of continuous care. Virtue is to work late into the night and to rise early in the morning to, as the British say, "get cracking" at the day's tasks. Meetings are piled upon meetings, obligations multiply like rabbits while an electric pressure pushes us to get our work done as soon as possible. With so much to do, napping or resting is downright sinful. The H-H Heresy is so deeply implanted that if we knew some magic word which would make sleep unnecessary, would not most of us use it?

Jesus, it seems, did not have to work overtime since He was fully aware of who really was working in and with and through Him. Even **He** did not have to save the world all by Himself! To remember what happened on that cushion in the stern of the boat provides a beautiful balance to all the admonitions of our Lord about being awake: "Be vigilant, be alert, watch always, you know not the hour, keep your lamps well oiled, stay awake . . . ." With Jesus, who
150

was caught napping Himself, we can look at these admonitions and see that we can also be vigilant by taking a nap, by being care-less and trustful.

Sleep, if we can remember its German mother-word meaning "loose," is also a form of Eastern prayer. Judo, the art of self-defense, grew out of the religious philosophy of the Tao. Judo is another form of "hanging loose." It is the art of self-defense by being un-tense, relaxed and care-less. "Ju" means "soft" and "do" means "art." They are combined into soft-art. As a means of self-defense, Judo is the art of letting the enemy destroy himself with his own attack force. Rather than standing firm and striking back, you move with the opponent's force and let that same angry force carry him to defeat. The Rabbi from Galilee meets the evil of the storm not with power, but with a simple "sh-sh, quiet." To the wonder of His friends, the storm suddenly subsides. Such power comes from living in holy communion with the Creator of storms and stillness.

Sleep is a time of rest and of re-creation. Sleep is like Christmas. It is both an expression of incarnation (we are human and not angels) and also a time to be gifted! The ancient singer of Psalm 126 worded it well:

> If the Lord does not build the house, in vain do its builders labor; if the Lord does not keep watch over the city, in vain does the watchman keep vigil. In vain is your earlier rising, your going to bed late to rest, you who toil for the bread you eat; when He pours gifts on His beloved while they slumber.

What gift does God pour out on those who slumber? Here we find (at the back door of sleep) another aspect of Siesta Spirituality. When we are care-less and at rest, there rises from the inner-person a release of creative ideas, solutions, and other such gifts. Remember what happened to Adam when he took a nap. He awoke to find that his prayer had been answered and indeed, what a beautiful answer he found! Or Joseph, husband to Mary, took his problems to bed with him and found that while asleep the solutions came to him: "Marry pregnant Mary (Mt 1:20) . . . take the child and his mother and flee the country to escape the wrath of King Herod" (Mt 2:13-14). Then there was Jacob and his night's adventure (Gen 32:23-33). Slumber is a gift-time, and we lack the space or the inclination to attempt to provide a psychological answer to this delightful mystery. Let mysteries be mysteries.

Not only do the holy books speak of sleep as gift-time, but fairy tales also speak of the same mystery. The tale of *Sleeping Beauty* attempts to teach the same message as Psalm 126. Stories like *Sleeping Beauty* encourage us not to fear passive periods in our lives. They say to us that quiet growth is also possible and is good growth. *Sleeping Beauty* holds a special charm for us in an overworked age in which we create so much smoke and noise when we work. We believe that with much smoke, noise and activity, things get done. The more activity and noise, the greater the production. We fear passive rest. We de-value times of withdrawal, prayer and meditation. The fairy tales are intended to reassure the child — the little girl and little boy in us — that periods of quiet withdrawal are good and that they are gift-times. We let go of control when we think only of ourselves (love thy self) and open our hearts to the Mystery. What we have need of is a new yellow road sign that we could hang on our door or place beside our chairs:

CAUTION
PERSON ASLEEP
GOD AT WORK

Having let go of control, we find ourselves being healed of various ills while being restored and recreated. The original story from which our modern *Sleeping Beauty* was created is the 14th or 15th century tale, "Sun, Moon and Talia." It was more exciting than *Sleeping Beauty* and was about a beautiful girl named Talia, who, under a curse, fell asleep for years in some deserted castle. A king comes by, finds her and makes love to her while she is asleep. Still asleep, she has twin children named Sun and Moon. Upon waking she finds her lover-king and her two beautiful children. This old tale concludes with the charming lines:

"Lucky people, so 'tis said,
Are blessed by Fortune whilst in bed."

Fairy tales, ancient Jewish prayer-songs, and the Gospel story by Mark all attempt to teach us what we find so hard to learn. As the pressure cooker of daily life perks away with both husband and wife working outside the home, with increasing responsibilities to church, community, family and self, we need to practice Siesta Spirituality. That such intermissions are prayer may seem strange at first. But remember that the official prayer of the Church for noon time called Sext means the same thing as siesta!

Naps in the middle of the day are not usually possible with our numerous responsibilities. But the spirit of siesta is possible in all our lives. There always are days off . . . and there are those times between supper and an evening event. If we are wise and "careless" like our Lord in the boat, we can just snooze off when the chance is present.

153

I hope that you have been reading this chapter in a comfortable easy chair and that by now you are convinced of the value of slumber spirituality. So without guilt and with rare expectation (for who knows how fortune and God will bless you), why not put down this book and turn off the light, turn the cosmos over to God and close your eyes . . . and pray a little?

A Prayer for Nap Time

(or for any time when we desire to be "out-of-control"
or to do "nothing-of-profit")

Well, Lord, it's not yet time to quit —
    all around me life is buzzing.
Nevertheless, I need to let go of being busy
    and, at times, just to relax.
May each nap time be a sacrament for me,
    giving me the grace to be aware
    that You are able
    to use stones to praise You
    and to raise up Your kingdom.

May my time of doing nothing — of letting go —
    remind me that it is You, my God,
    who is bringing about the kingdom
    and that the more I can let You do it —
    especially in the midst of my greatest efforts —

the more beautifully and gracefully
the age of justice and peace
can come to this tired world.
Show to me that if I can let go
of trying to control people, events
and especially my futile attempts at controlling You,
holiness will flow to me more quickly and surely.
May each short time of leisure
renew my spirit,
fill my heart with insights
and restore my body.

As Your Son, Jesus, let go of His cares
and fell asleep in the storm-tossed boat,
may I now let go of my cares and rest in You,
my beloved God and ever-vigilant lover.

Amen+

The Sacred Silk Drum

As we come to the last chapter of this book, we keep in mind that all good prayer leads to following in the footsteps of Jesus. When we do that, we are indeed the people of the "Way." Those who follow the compassionate Lord must themselves be compassionate to all. The Christian life is not one of simply prayer, worship and devotion, but also a life of service, of justice and dedication to peace. Works of mercy and justice are to be the overflow of our lives and not the giving of our last drop of energy. Justice and mercy, compassionate service and the pursuit of peace will overflow from hearts that pray all ways and always. We strive to love God with all of our hearts, with all our strength and with all our souls, and in such totality of loving find the fullness of Life.

When asked about the totality of loving, a wholeness of love that includes not only God but self and neighbor, Jesus tells a story. It is a famous story about a man who fell in with thugs who beat him, robbed him, and left him half-dead along the roadside (Lk 10:25-37). This parable is more than a story about adventure and compassion on the highway. It is, indeed, a classic story. But like many of the other parables, our hearts are dulled by the frequent repetition of it so that we fail to unravel its silver thread. It is a parable and not a moral story about helping strangers in need. We must ask ourselves the question, "Why?" Why does the traveling salesman from Samaria act differently than the priest and Levite; differently from the butcher, baker or candlestick maker? Jesus' parable is more than some clever answer to the difficult question, "Who is my neighbor?" It is also a statement-story about how to love with a totality of energy. Different behavior, like that of the traveling man from Samaria, happens in the lives of people when they are prayerful and free.

Free of normal fears, they are able to respond to the events of life in a different way than other people. Being free of "What-you-shouldn't-do," they are then able to do "What-you-should-do." A thousand-and-one explanations might be given for why the priest and the levite in the parable failed to stop to be of assistance. You and I have as many reasons for the narrowness of our own loving and compassionate service to those in need. But what was it that caused the Samaritan to stop and be compassionate, to inconvenience himself — yes, and even to endanger himself?

Remember the famous lines of Henry Thoreau? It was a quotation frequently heard during the late 1960's: "If a man does not keep pace with his companions, perhaps it is because he hears a different drummer. Let him step to the music which he hears, however measured or far away." The Samaritan, one of a class of people for whom the Jews had great animosity, seemed to hear a different drummer — as his compassionate behavior reveals. Since the man in the ditch was a Jew, his social and religious enemy, his care of the man was beyond the call of ordinary kindness. He heard a different drum, and so his behavior on that deserted road to Jericho wasn't heroic; it was only plain and natural. Natural, you ask? Yes, natural for someone whose heart heard and saw what the others did not. But, lest we become entangled in words that speak only to the head, perhaps we should follow the excellent example of Jesus and find our answer in another story. I would like to share with you an old Japanese story called "The Silk Drum."

Once upon a time, long ago in ancient Japan, there lived a mighty lord who realized that his death was very near. He urged his only daughter, the Lady Yumiyo, that she should marry. He said to her, "Dearest daughter, the green of the plum trees has come and gone and it is the time of the blossoms. But you, dear one, still have not chosen a husband. All those men who have come for your hand you have dismissed. Am I, your father, to die without seeing you married and without seeing my grandchildren?"

His daughter replied, "No, father, for I shall fashion a drum of silk which will be stretched over a bamboo frame. The man who hears the note when my fingers strike the drum, that man will I marry."

"What foolishness!" said the old man. "A silk drum does not make any sound. Poor me, I shall die without seeing my grandchildren." But the Lady Yumiyo was as strong-willed as she was beautiful, and so the silk drum was made. Many young men came to listen to her drum, because she was not only beautiful but also very rich. But, alas, when she played upon her silk drum not a sound did any of them hear. The months and seasons passed, as a long procession of suitors came and went. The aged lord mumbled, "Oh, I told you so, I told you so!"

Then one day, into the courtyard came a young, handsome and richly-dressed man. He had about him the air of one who had traveled long and far. He made a deep bow to the aged lord and a lesser but gentle one to the Lady Yumiyo who sat with her silk drum at her side.

"From where do you come, youthful stranger?" asked the father.

"From beyond the mountains and the seas; from far, far away," replied the youthful stranger.

"And for what, may I ask, have you traveled such a great distance?" asked the father.

"My Lord," said the young man, " I have come to marry your daughter."

"She is only for the man who can hear her silk drum. Do not tell me that you have heard its sound in your far-off kingdom, across the mountains and the seas?"

The young man answered, "You are correct, my Lord, no sound of the drum has reached me."

"Then, stranger," said the father, "be on your way, like all the others before you. Why do you even linger here?"

"Because, my Lord," said the young stranger, "I hear its silence."

And the Lady Yumiyo smiled and put away her silken drum, since she had no further use for it.

The Samaritan in the story that was told by Jesus heard a silken drum. Its sound is the absence of all sound. It can be heard not only across vast mountain ranges and seas, but even beyond time and space! Those who hear the silk drum of heaven do indeed, as Henry Thoreau said, keep a different pace than their companions. But you and I, like the frustrated suitors in the old Japanese story, are eager to love God and strain our ears to hear a divine voice. And when we fail to hear anything, when we fail to see anything, we express our religious dilemma and are told, "You must have faith. You must learn to believe in that which you cannot see, touch or hear." Such pious

160

sounding advice only sets our feet to an arid pathway. For how can we ever learn to love with such a totality of energy — with all our heart, all our soul and all our strength — *unless* we do hear, see and feel? Can we, like the young stranger in the old Japanese story, hear the "silence" of the sacred silk drum? Can we hear the voice of God in its very silence? Can we feel the intimate touch of the Divine Lover in the presence of every touch?

If we desire to love with such a totality and to express that love by living in prayerful unity with the Divine Mystery, then two things will be necessary. First, we will keep in mind that the God we believe in is the God we will experience. For example, if we believe in a God who is a strict judge, an almighty judge who acts like some character from a Charles Dickens' novel who punishes his children so that they will be good, then that will be the God we will experience. That will be the God we will pray to for mercy and forgiveness. As a result of such a belief, our lives will be measured by the drumbeat of laws, regulations and obligations. We will live in fear, and our prayer will be that of pleading for mercy. Or, if we believe that the Divine Presence speaks to us in a fiery volcanic voice or in shimmering lights in the night, then we will never hear the "real" voice of our God. But, if we believe that God does indeed play upon a silken drum, plays upon it with a lover's fingers, then the strongest proof for the existence of God will be the absence of God! And then, in that "silent, silken void," our daily lives will be filled — no, rather crowded and over-flowing — with experiences of God.

If we desire to become persons who love with such an intensity, with whole hearts and minds, the second point we need to keep in mind is that we will never hear the silence of the Sacred Silk Drum unless we learn to sit still. We must learn how to sit peacefully in order to quiet the inner noise as well as the external racket of our lives. Those persons whose lives are full of constant noise, who are unable to listen and find it necessary to be constantly talking, these can never be lovers of one another or of the gods. If we wish to learn how to pray all ways and always, then we must learn the art of listening. Listening — not simply patiently pausing until the other person is finished speaking so that we can speak — is truly hearing with a heart that is quiet and at peace. We have spoken in this book about praying with the eyes, with the nose and with our feet as well as the rest of our bodies. We pray best of all with our ears when we learn the art of listening. Those who have learned the art of stillness are gifted not only with an inner peace but with rich experiences . . . the wonder-filled ones of God. As George Eliot wrote: "If we had a keen vision of all that is ordinary in human life, it would be like hearing the grass grow or the squirrel's heart beat, and we should die of that roar which is the other side of silence."

The ancient ones believed that no one could see God and live. Perhaps we cannot hear God without the risk of dying from the roar, which is the "other" side of the Great Silence. While no one has seen God, we mortals have, over the long centuries, fashioned a variety of images of the Diving Presence. One of particular interest is an image that is traditional in India. It is the image of God as the Lord Shiva. The Lord Shiva is called the Lord of the Dance. He stands on one foot, balanced as some ballet dancer, and in one hand the Lord holds a drum! God plays upon his sacred drum as everything in the cosmos dances to its beat — stars and comets, squirrels and oceans, birds on the wind and snow-capped mountains — everything, that is, but we mortals, for we do not know how to listen to Shiva's drum! Those who hear the

Lord's drum are those who are able to pray all ways and always. For prayer is not some pious pathway to find God. No, prayer is the expression, the music, the dance of those who have found God! Only those who are lovers, those who have learned to be artists of silence, only they, like the traveling salesman from Samaria, can respond to the Lord's Silken Sacred Drum. They move to its melody and their dance is called . . . prayer. With graceful step, they move in perfect harmony with all the rest of creation . . . praying, dancing, all ways.

A Prayer for Praying All Ways

Lord, who among us
    can pray always?
The practical things of life —
    beds to be made, meals to be prepared,
    a job to be held down, cars to be repaired —
    these demand that I not spend all my time
    on my knees before You.
Show to me, Ever-Present God,
    how I can pray all ways and at all times,
    and so, pray always.
Reveal to me, Lord,
    that nothing is foreign to You,
    who are the creator of all that is,
    and since all things have come from You,
    the very use of them, with awareness,
    can be the very truest of prayers.

Help me to be awake
    to Your continuous movement about me:
    in all the actions of creation,
    in all the dynamics of discovery;
    in work and play,
    love and study,
    within sleep and music,
    feasting and fasting.
May I strive each day to expand the limits
    of my times of prayer
    until that blessed time when each hour —
    day or night, asleep as well as awake —
    will be spent in awareness of the Mystery.

With gratitude and praise,
    in petition and adoration,
    in a living communion,
    I aspire to live my life
    praying all ways and always.
I make this prayer in the name of Your Son, Jesus,
    who lives with You and the Holy Spirit,
    forever and ever.

Amen+

the author

Edward Hays is a Midwesterner and a Catholic priest. He is presently the director of a contemplative house of prayer, Shantivanam. His life has been enriched by his many years as a teacher and as a pastor. His seven years as pastor with the American Indians, the Pottawatomies of Kansas, was a time of education concerning the sacredness of all life. His philosophy of life has also been shaped by his travels to the Near East and India and his experiences in the Orient. These experiences together with his love of art and of storytelling blend to form a background for his writing and personal life.